I0020395

MICROSOFT WORD 2019
IN 90 PAGES

by **Beth Brown**

Belleyre Books

Copyright © 2019 Beth Brown

All rights reserved. No part of this publication may be reproduced, scanned, or distributed in any printed or electronic form without written consent from the author. The author is the sole owner of the content presented within this text. Photographs copyright Beth Brown.

Published by Belleyre Books
www.belleyrebooks.com

First Edition

ISBN 978-0-9986844-4-4 paperback
ISBN 978-0-9986844-5-1 eBook

Complimentary examination copies are available for educational institutions. Please inquire through www.belleyrebooks.com/order.

This text is in no way connected with Microsoft Corporation.

Microsoft and Microsoft Word are either registered trademarks of the Microsoft Corporation in the United States and/or other countries. Screen shots and icons used with permission from Microsoft.

Names of all other products mentioned herein are used for identification purposes only and may be trademarks of their respective owners.

This book was created using Microsoft Word 365.

Revision_1

Also Available

MICROSOFT WORD 2016 IN 90 PAGES

MICROSOFT EXCEL 2016 IN 90 PAGES

MICROSOFT POWERPOINT 2016 IN 90 PAGES

Table of Contents

Tables

Preface

The goal of this book is to provide an approachable learning experience for Word 2019. Through step-by-step directions, informative tables, and numerous screenshots, you'll be able to master Word 2019 to create professional, effective documents that communicate exactly what you intend.

Microsoft Word 2019 in 90 Pages is written for Microsoft Word 2019 that runs on Windows 10. This text is compatible with Word 365 but may not cover all 365 features.

How to Use this Book

Chapters divide the features of Word into related topics with step-by-step instructions for each concept. You can apply these directions to a new document or an existing one. References are made throughout the chapters to tables that further detail commands, actions, and features related to a concept.

Refer to the last page of this book for a tear-out Word 2019 Quick Reference with step-by-step instructions that are keyed to the text. For more information, visit www.belleyrebooks.com.

Accessibility Note

Keyboard shortcuts allow you to keep your hands on the keyboard for faster document development. Some keyboards shortcuts are faster and easier than trying to perform the same action with the mouse. In these cases, the keyboard shortcut is explicitly provided in the instructions.

Word is an accessible application, and therefore, keyboard shortcuts are provided for essentially every possible command and action. You can determine these shortcuts by viewing the pop-up ScreenTips (pg. 6) and by typing "keyboard shortcuts" into the Tell Me search box (pg. 4). Further, pressing the Alt key once displays keyboard shortcuts for navigating the tabs and commands on the Ribbon.

About the Author

Beth Brown is the author of more than 40 computer science and computer applications textbooks. An engineering graduate of Florida Atlantic University, Ms. Brown holds a B.S. in Computer Science. She has worked with students and educators worldwide to develop Microsoft Office curriculum materials in addition to her work in programming, research and development, technical writing, and business.

Chapter 1
The Basics

Microsoft Word 2019 is the ubiquitous word processor application of the Microsoft Office 2019 productivity suite. Word is used to publish documents: letters, flyers, brochures, books, eBooks, and many, many other forms of communication that will be printed, emailed, or read onscreen. Learning Word is essential to anyone who works in an office, goes to school, or uses a PC, laptop, tablet, or mobile device to create documents.

Starting Word

How you start Word will depend on your device, but you will usually need to click the Word 2019 icon in the Taskbar at the bottom of a PC screen or double-click the icon on the Desktop. If you don't see the Word icon on your computer, click the Start menu in the lower-left corner of your screen and scroll through the list to locate the Word 2019 icon. Click this icon to start Word.

TIP Press the Windows key to the left of the spacebar to display the Start menu.

The Word Interface

The Word *application interface* refers to the area where you interact with Word. When you start Word, the interface, also called the Word window, displays the Start screen where you can choose to create a new file or open an existing file.

In the Start screen (Figure 1, pg. 2), click Blank document or Single spaced (blank) to create a new document. Or, click a link under Recent to open a file you've already created.

The Word window with a new document looks similar to Figure 2, pg. 2. Refer to Table 1 on pg. 3 for information about the features.

Figure 1 The Start screen.

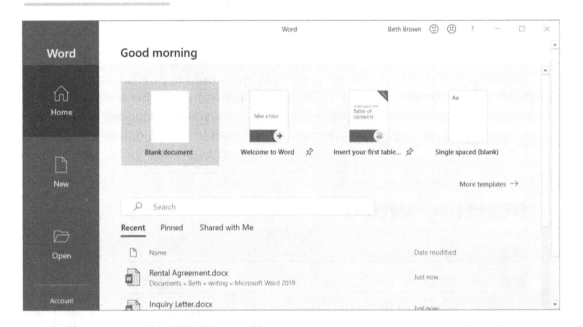

Figure 2 A new document window.

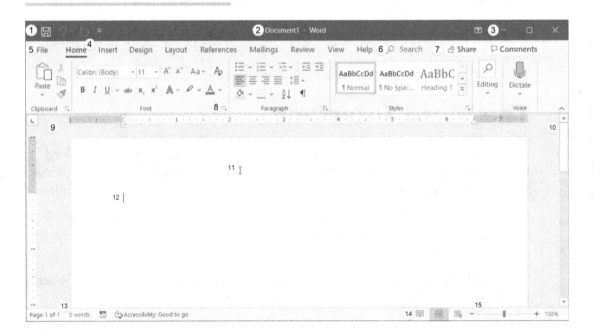

Table 1 The Word Window

① **Quick Access Toolbar**	Save, Undo, Redo, Customize Quick Access Toolbar Refer also to pg. 18.
② **File name**	Document1 is the default file name until you save your document with a more descriptive name.
③ **Window controls**	Minimize ▬ and Restore 🗗 window size. Close the window with the X button ✕.
④ **Ribbon**	The Ribbon is divided into tabs that group commands (File, Home, Insert, Design, Layout, References, Mailings, Review, View, and Help). Click the Ribbon Display Options button 🖽, near the window controls, to hide the Ribbon or reduce the Ribbon to tabs only.
⑤ **File tab**	Click to display the Backstage view where you can open, close, save as, print, and distribute your document. Refer also to pg. 7.
⑥ **Tell Me box**	A help and search feature. Refer to pg. 4.
⑦ **Share and Comments**	Collaborate with others on a document. See and respond to comments. Refer to Chapter 7.
⑧ **Dialog box launcher** ⌐	Click to display a dialog box with the options for a Ribbon group.
⑨ **Rulers**	Displays document dimensions. Use to align objects and to set indents, tab stops, margins, and table column widths.
⑩ **Scroll bar**	Drag the scroll box or click scroll arrows to bring unseen parts of your document into view.
⑪ **I-beam pointer**	Mouse pointer shape when the mouse pointer is on the document. Refer to pgs. 5 – 7.
⑫ **Insertion point**	Position where typed characters appear. Refer to pg. 5.

⑬ **Page and Word statistics**	Click the word count for more information.
⑭ **Document views**	Click an icon to change the way a document is viewed. Refer to pg. 9 and Chapter 7.
⑮ **Zoom**	Drag the slider or click – or + to change document magnification.

TIP To customize the Ribbon, click File ⇨ Options ⇨ Customize Ribbon.

The Most Important Word Feature

The Tell Me box is probably the most important Word feature to know about. It is a powerful search and help tool that appears after the last Ribbon tab. It's symbolized by a magnifying glass with the text Search (Figure 3).

Figure 3 The Tell Me box.

When you click Search and then type a word or phrase, Word suggests related commands (Figure 4).

Figure 4 Search text in the Tell Me box displays a menu of options.

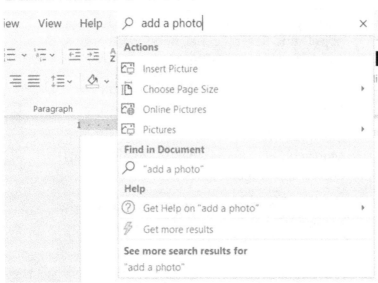

The Tell Me results menu is context sensitive. Different commands and actions will be displayed depending on what's going on in your document.

At the bottom of the Tell Me results menu, there are options to display Help and perform a Smart Lookup. These commands open a *pane* with a set of options. To close the pane, you click Close X in the upper-right corner.

The Tell Me box is the most important Word feature because you no longer have to remember which tab holds a Ribbon command or which button is which — you can just get to work and ask Word for whatever it is you need.

TIP Use the Index in the back of this book to quickly locate information for a Word feature.

TIP Refer to the tear-out Quick Reference at the back of the book for step-by-step instructions for commonly performed actions.

Communicating with Word

Input devices are needed so that you can communicate with Word. The devices you are most likely to use are the keyboard and mouse.

As you type on the keyboard, characters appear in your document at the location of the blinking line called the *insertion point*:

Text appears at the blinking insertion point.|

Special keys on the keyboard are used to control the insertion point position, while the Escape key allows you to cancel an action, such as the display of a dialog box. The Ctrl key is used in combination with other keys to perform an action. Refer to Table 2.

Table 2 Keyboard Keys and their Functions

Esc	Press the Escape (Esc) key to cancel the current action.
Ctrl	Press and hold the Control (Ctrl) key before pressing a second key. For example, Ctrl+S means to press and hold Ctrl while pressing the S key once.

↑ ← ↓ →	Press an arrow key to position the insertion point. Press Ctrl+arrow key to move the insertion point from word to word or line to line.
Home	Press Home to move the insertion to the beginning of a line. Ctrl+Home moves the insertion point to the beginning of a document.
End	Press End to move the insertion point to the end of a line. Ctrl+End moves the insertion point to the end of a document.
Page Up Page Down	The Page Up (PgUp) and Page Down (PgDn) keys are used to scroll a document. Ctrl+Page Up scrolls to the top of the previous page. Ctrl+Page Down moves to the top of the next page.
Delete	Press the Delete key to remove the character to the right of the insertion point.
←Backspace	The Backspace key removes the character to the left of the insertion point.

The mouse is a pointing device that displays a graphic image called a *pointer*. You can use the mouse to select commands on the Ribbon, respond to prompts, position the insertion point, and edit text. When you rest (hover) the mouse pointer on a command or feature of the interface a helpful *ScreenTip* pops up, as shown in Figure 5.

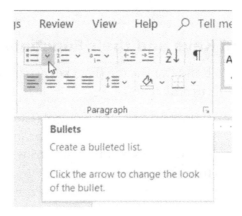

Figure 5 A ScreenTip.

The pointer shape changes depending on where the pointer is placed. One exception is when Word is working on an action, which is indicated by an hourglass pointer. You can further communicate with Word with different actions through the mouse buttons. Refer to Table 3.

Table 3 Mouse Actions and Pointer Shapes

Point	Move the mouse until the pointer is placed on an object or in a specific area.
Click	Press and release the left mouse button once.
Double-click	Press and release the left mouse button twice in rapid succession.
Right-click	Press and release the right mouse button once.
Drag	Press and hold the left mouse button while moving the mouse. This action positions an object or highlights text.
Scroll wheel	If available, rotate the scroll wheel to move a document up or down to bring unseen parts into view.
⌖	The arrow pointer is displayed when the mouse pointer is positioned over a command or another clickable object.
I	The I-beam pointer is displayed when the mouse pointer is positioned within a document. Click to move the insertion point to the position of the I-beam.
✥	The four-headed arrow pointer appears when you point to an object, such as an image. Refer to Chapter 4.
⤢	The two-headed arrow pointer appears when you point to a handle of a selected object. Drag the handle with this pointer to size the object.
👆	The hand shape is typical when the mouse pointer is positioned over a hyperlink. Click to follow a link.

The Backstage View

The File tab on the Word Ribbon displays the *Backstage view*. From here, you work with files, print, and set Word options, among other things. Click the Back arrow ← when you want to return to your document. Click a command on the left side of the Backstage view screen to bring up related options:

New displays options for creating a new document.

Open displays links to recently opened files. Click Browse in the Open screen to display a dialog box where you can navigate to files not listed.

Save is discussed in the next section. Save As is used to save a document copy with a new name. If you want to save the copy in a new location, click Browse and then navigate to the desired folder in the Save As dialog box. You also have the option of changing the file format to PDF or another file type when you use save as.

Print displays a print preview with options for selecting your printer and changing print settings.

Share displays options for emailing your document or making it available to others for editing or viewing. Click Email for options to send your document as a Word attachment or as a PDF (the recommended method if you do not want changes made to your document).

Export has options for creating a PDF. There are also options for converting your document to a different file type. For example, you may need a plain text file with no formatting. When a file is exported, the original remains, and a new file is created.

Transform is used to convert a document to a web page.

Close removes your document from the Word window without closing Word.

Options displays the Word Options dialog box for customizing how Word interacts with you. With this dialog box you can modify auto save, AutoCorrect, display options, the Ribbon, and the Quick Access Toolbar.

Viewing a Document

There are a few different ways to view your document onscreen. Print Layout is the default and is usually best when actively working on a document. You can see exactly how a document will look when printed by using this view. A document is typically already displayed in this view, but you can click View ⇨ Print Layout if necessary.

View ⇨ Side to Side changes the page movement in Page Layout view. When you have this option selected, you will use the horizontal scroll bar to navigate from page to page, moving left to right through your document. View ⇨ Vertical is the default option.

Read Mode fills the screen with your document and provides navigational arrows for scrolling through the text. It is best used when you want to read a long document. Click View ⇨ Read Mode to view a document this way.

View ⇨ Web Layout shows you how a document will appear as a web page.

Buttons on the Status bar at the bottom of the Word window can also be used to change views (Figure 6). If the buttons are not displayed, customize your Status bar by right-clicking in the Status bar and then clicking View Shortcuts.

Figure 6 The Read Mode, Print Layout, and Web Layout button on the Status bar.

TIP Refer to pg. 79 for more information on viewing a document. See pg. 84 for information about outline view.

Saving a Document

You will want to save your document frequently — every minute or two if you're doing a lot of typing and editing. Saving often is so important that Word provides several ways to execute the action:

- The Save command on the File tab. However, this is a rather weighty way to have to get to a command you want to execute often.

- The Save button 🖫 on the Quick Access Toolbar (Figure 2, pg. 2). The first time this button is clicked for a new document, you will see the Backstage view where you can navigate to the appropriate location for the file. Clicking 🖫 with a named document simply updates the file with your changes without showing the Backstage view.

- And if you want to keep your hands on the keyboard, press Ctrl+S to save your document (press and hold the Ctrl key and then press the S key once).

Quitting Word

If you are ready to quit Word and close the application interface, click Close X in the upper-right corner of the Word window. If you've made unsaved changes to an open document, you will be prompted to either save or discard the changes before quitting.

Chapter 2
Creating a New Document

Creating a new document involves starting Word, choosing a new document type, setting up your document page size and orientation, and then typing your content.

First Things First

Choosing a New Document Template

Whether you're at the Word Start screen or the File ⇨ New screen, you'll need to decide which template you want to use for your new document. A *template* is a document that already has some formatting. When you create a new document, you are using a supplied Word template. The Word Blank document template uses a 1.15 line spacing and adds space after each paragraph. The Single spaced (blank) template uses single spacing for lines and no spacing after a paragraph.

TIP Chapter 7, pg. 87 explains how to create your own templates.

Changing Page Size and Orientation

After deciding on the template to use, you will need to customize the page size and orientation, if necessary. Is your document a standard 8½" x 11"? Or are you creating a postcard mailer? The default page size is letter (8.5" x 11"). Are you creating a flyer or certificate that requires a landscape orientation (horizontal)? The default is portrait orientation (vertical).

To create a new document and customize your page size and orientation:

1. Start Word and click Blank document.
2. *Optional.* To change the page size, click Layout ⇨ Size and then click the appropriate size from the list.
3. *Optional.* To change the page orientation, click Layout ⇨ Orientation and then click either Portrait or Landscape.

Typing Text

The key to professional-looking word processor documents depends on two rules:

1. **Press the Enter key only at the end of a paragraph.**
2. **Type one space, and only one space, after a period.**

Pressing Enter only at the end of a paragraph allows a process called *word wrap* to determine when to move text to the next line. By allowing word wrap to break lines of text, your text will best fit the width of the page and you will avoid complications later if you add or remove text.

Word carefully adjusts characters and words to fit proportionately on a line. If you type two spaces after a period, you end up with distracting gaps that vary in width. For a better reading experience and an overall professional impression, use only one space after a period.

TIP Typing the content for your document can be easier with a close-up view. Use the Zoom controls in the Status bar to change the magnification of your document. Click + to increase the magnification, click – to reduce; or drag the slider in either direction. Click 100% to display the Zoom dialog box. Note that 100% displays text close to actual size; however, the magnification does not affect the size of the text when printed.

TIP MLA formatting requires one space after the period, while APA recommends two spaces after the period for easier draft reading.

Displaying Formatting Marks

When typing, it is helpful to display the hidden symbols used to represent paragraph marks, spaces, and tabs (Figure 7). Showing all characters can help you avoid typos, such as two spaces in a row. To display *formatting marks*, click Home ⇨ ¶ (Show/Hide ¶).

Figure 7 Formatting marks.

The·most·common·formatting·marks·appear·as·a·dot·to·represent·a·space·and·

an·arrow· → for·a·tab.·The·paragraph·mark·is·called·a·pilcrow.¶

The Soft Return

When you press Enter, you insert a *hard return* into your text. The *soft return* is a character used to end a line and move the insertion point to the next while still maintaining the same paragraph. The soft return, sometimes called a *newline*, is created by pressing Shift+Enter. You use a soft return when you want to move related information to the next line without adding extra space between lines. For example, a soft return is used to break a title over two lines without adding additional space between lines.

Spelling and Grammar Checking

As you type, Word checks for spelling errors by comparing text to a dictionary file. When a combination of characters appears similar to a word in the dictionary, the AutoCorrect feature automatically makes changes. For example, "acn" will automatically be changed to "can". To customize corrections, click File ⇨ Options ⇨ Proofing ⇨ AutoCorrect Options.

When even AutoCorrect doesn't recognize a combination of characters, Word alerts you to a possible spelling error by displaying a red squiggly line.

To correct a red flagged word or phrase (spelling error):

1. Right-click the text. A menu is displayed similar to Figure 8.

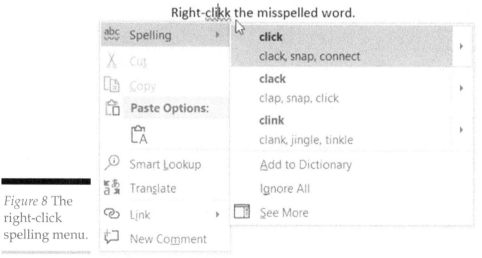

Figure 8 The right-click spelling menu.

2. Click a correctly spelled word to replace the unknown word.
    Or

Click Ignore All to remove the squiggly line from this and every occurrence of the spelling in the document.

Or

Click Add to Dictionary to remove the squiggly line and add the word to the dictionary file so that it will be recognized in all future Word documents.

TIP AutoCorrect is often very helpful for typos, but at times it can cause some oddly worded text. To reverse an AutoCorrect action, press Ctrl+Z immediately after it happens. Alternatively, you can point to a corrected word and then click the blue bar to display AutoCorrect options.

A sentence that doesn't follow grammar rules will be flagged with a blue double line.

To correct a blue flagged word or phrase (grammar error):

1. Right-click the text. A menu is displayed similar to Figure 9.

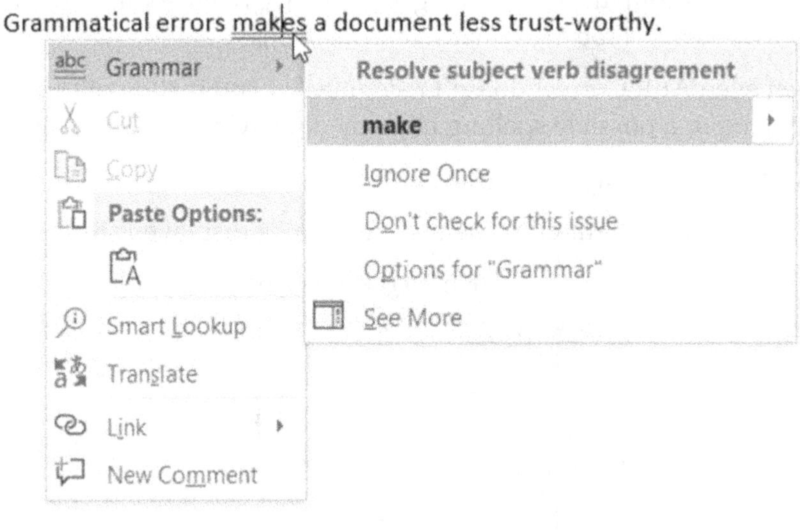

Grammatical errors makes a document less trust-worthy.

abc	Grammar	▶		Resolve subject verb disagreement
✕	Cut			**make** ▶
	Copy			Ignore Once
	Paste Options:			Don't check for this issue
	A			Options for "Grammar"
	Smart Lookup			See More
	Translate			
	Link	▶		
	New Comment			

Figure 9 The right-click grammar menu.

2. Click a word or phrase to replace the flagged text.

Or

Click Ignore Once to remove the blue double line from this occurrence.

Or

Click Options for "Grammar" to display the Grammar Settings dialog box.

TIP To modify grammar settings, click File ⇨ Options ⇨ Proofing and then click a Writing Style option. Click Settings to further customize Writing Style.

TIP To process all spelling and grammar issues at once, click Spelling and Grammar Check ⬚ in the Status bar or click Review ⇨ Editor ⬚ (may also be Check Document or Spelling & Grammar). In the Editor task pane, click Spelling or Grammar. Next, click Ignore or select a replacement and click Change to resolve an issue and move to the next one. When the review is complete, a dialog box displays the Flesch Readability scores and other statistics.

Inserting Special Characters

When you need to type a character or symbol that isn't on the keyboard, such as á or ¢, you use Insert ⇨ Symbol (Figure 10).

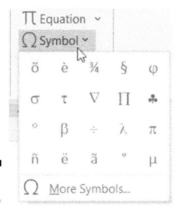

Figure 10 The Symbol menu.

Click a symbol to insert it into the document at the insertion point or click More Symbols to display a dialog box with additional symbols and special characters, including nonbreaking hyphens and spaces and em (—) and en (-) dashes. Change the Font and Subset in the dialog box for different sets of characters.

Some symbols can be created by typing character sequences that are recognized by the AutoCorrect feature. For example, typing 1/4 displays ¼. (c) converts to © and, similarly, (tm) automatically converts to ™. For a full list of conversions, click File ⇨ Options ⇨ Proofing ⇨ AutoCorrect Options.

Although not technically a special character, the Date & Time command, also on the Insert tab, is worth mentioning. It inserts a time stamp at the insertion point. The time stamp is a field code that updates when you open the document. You can also click the code and press F9 to update it.

Some accented and special characters can be inserted using Ctrl key sequences before typing the character. Refer to Table 4 below.

Table 4 Ctrl Key Sequences for Special Characters

Ctrl+` *letter*	À, à, È, è, Ì, ì, Ò, ò, Ù, ù
Ctrl+' *letter*	Á, á, É, é, Í, í, Ó, ó, Ú, ú, Ý, ý
Ctrl+Shift+^ *letter*	Â, â, Ê, ê, Î, î, Ô, ô, Û, û
Ctrl+Shift+~ *letter*	Ã, ã, Ñ, ñ, Õ, õ
Ctrl+Shift+: *letter*	Ä, ä, Ë, ë, Ï, ï, Ö, ö, Ü, ü, Ÿ, ÿ
Ctrl+Shift+@ A, a	Å, å
Ctrl+Shift+& A, a	Æ, æ
Ctrl+Shift+& O, o	Œ, œ
Ctrl+, C, c	Ç, ç
Ctrl+' D, d	Đ, ð
Ctrl+/ O, o	Ø, ø
Ctrl+Alt+Shift+?	¿
Ctrl+Alt+Shift+!	¡
Ctrl+Shift+& s	ß

Typing Hyperlinks

Inserting an active link into your document is as easy as typing it. Word interprets text such as @, .com, and www. as part of a hyperlink and automatically converts the text into a link. Selected text can also be formatted by clicking Insert ⇨ Link. If you distribute the file as a Word document or as a PDF, the viewer will be able to click the links in your document to follow them.

To reverse an unwanted hyperlink conversion, click Undo on the Quick Access Toolbar (Ctrl+Z), or right-click the link and select Remove Hyperlink. To convert text that wasn't automatically converted, right-click and select Link to display a dialog box where you specify Link to, Text to display, and Address information.

Editing Text

Edits to your document are almost always required to attain a polished, effective message. Editing involves adding, deleting, and moving text.

To edit the text in your document:

1. Click Home ⇨ ¶ (Show/Hide ¶) to display formatting marks, if they are not already displayed.

2. Click the I-beam pointer or use the arrow keys to place the insertion point at the position to make the edit.

3. If you want to add text, then type the new text. It is entered at the insertion point.

4. If you want to delete, duplicate, or move text, first *select*, or highlight, the block of text.

    Selecting text is the process of dragging the mouse over text to highlight it, as in Figure 11. (Refer to Table 5, pg. 18, for other methods to select text.) If you need to clear the selection, click anywhere outside the highlighted text.

    Figure 11 A selected block of text.

    A·selected·block·of·text·is·displayed·as·highlighted.¶

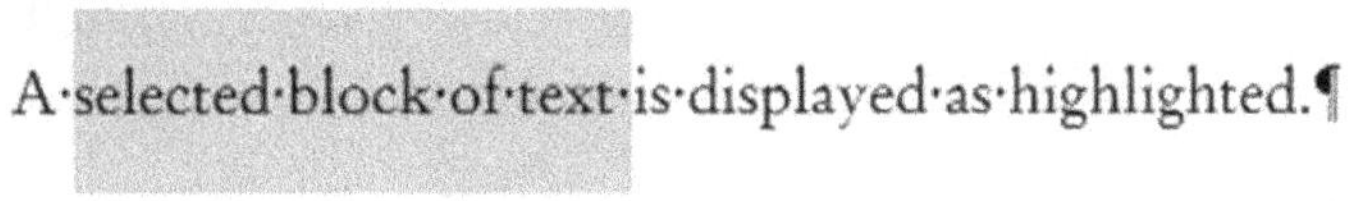

5. If you want to delete the block of text, press the Delete key. The text is removed.

6. If you want to move the block of text, click Home ⇨ Cut. The text is removed from the document. Next, place the insertion point where you want to insert the cut block and then click Home ⇨ Paste. The block is moved.

7. If you want to duplicate the block of text, click Home ⇨ Copy. The text is copied, leaving the original in place. Next, place the insertion point where you want to insert the copied block and then click Home ⇨ Paste. The block is duplicated.

8. Save (Ctrl+S) your document often during the editing process!

TIP When text is selected with the mouse, a mini toolbar appears with formatting options. The mini toolbar is discussed in Chapter 3.

There are many ways to edit text (Table 5 below). Editing commands are in the upper-left of the Word window, in the Quick Access Toolbar, and on the Home tab, as shown in Figure 12. The Cut and Copy commands place selected text onto the *Clipboard*, a storage area in memory, for use later.

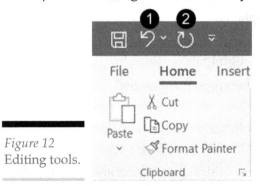

Figure 12
Editing tools.

Table 5 Editing Features

① **Undo**	Click to remove the most recently typed text. Click the Undo arrow to choose from a list of actions to reverse.
② **Repeat Typing**	Click to reverse the last Undo.
Home ⇨ Cut	Click Cut (Ctrl+X) to remove selected text and place it onto the Clipboard.
Home ⇨ Copy	Click Copy (Ctrl+C) to place a duplicate of selected text onto the Clipboard, leaving the original text unchanged.
Home ⇨ Paste	Click Paste (Ctrl+V) to place the last cut or copied text at the insertion point. After pasting, click Paste Options to control formats (pg. 31).
Home ⇨ Clipboard dialog box launcher	Click the Clipboard group dialog box launcher to open the Clipboard task pane. Click an item on the Clipboard to place it at the insertion point.
Block selection	Drag the I-beam pointer from the first character to the last to select a block of text.

Word selection	Double-click the I-beam pointer on a word to select the word and the space after.
Paragraph selection	Triple-click in text to select the entire paragraph, including the paragraph marker.
Character selection from the insertion point	Press and hold the Shift key while pressing an arrow key to select text starting from the insertion point.
Word selection from the insertion point	Press and hold the Shift and Ctrl keys together while pressing an arrow key to select one word at time starting from the insertion point.
Block selection from the insertion point	Press and hold the Shift key and then click the I-beam pointer to select all the text from the insertion point to the point clicked.
Line selection from the insertion point	Press Shift+Home to select text from the insertion point to the beginning of the line; Shift+End to select to the end of the line.
Vertical block selection	Press and hold the Alt key while dragging in any direction.
Sentence selection	Press and hold the Ctrl key while clicking anywhere in a sentence.
⤴	Point to the left of text until the pointer changes to the right arrow shape and then click to select the line of text to the right. Drag the right arrow pointer to select multiple lines of text. Double-click to select the paragraph. Triple-click to select the entire document.
Home ⇨ Select ⇨ Select All	Click Select All to select the entire document.
←Backspace	Press to remove a character to the left of the insertion point or to remove a selected block of text.
Delete	Press to remove a character to the right of the insertion point or to remove a selected block of text.
Shift+F5	Press to return to the last edit.

Changing, Finding, and Choosing Your Words

Choosing the right words is imperative for any communication, and Word has the tools you need.

Thesaurus

The first of these is the *thesaurus*, which is used to replace a word with a synonym that is similar in meaning.

To find an alternative word:

1. Right-click the word you want to change. A menu is displayed.

2. Click Synonym and then click a word from the displayed list.

   Or

   Click Synonym ⇨ Thesaurus to open a task pane where you can further explore the meaning and replacement choices of a word.

Search and Replace

The second tool is search and replace, which finds a word and replaces it with another that you have specified. To make word replacements:

1. Click Home ⇨ Replace. A dialog box is displayed.

2. Type the text to look for in the Find what box and the replacement text in the Replace with box, similar to Figure 13.

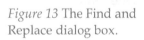

Figure 13 The Find and Replace dialog box.

3. Click Find Next to find your search text.

4. Click Replace to edit the occurrence and then automatically search for the next occurrence.

5. Continue clicking Replace until the entire document has been searched.

TIP Use the Replace All button with caution as you may make unexpected changes.

To further refine your search, click More to display search options (Figure 14).

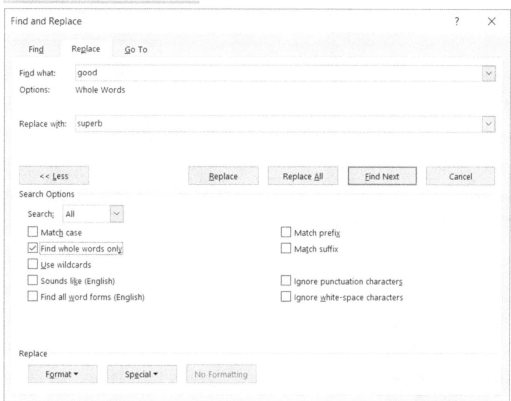

Figure 14 The More options in the Find and Replace dialog box.

The search specified in Figure 14 will locate only the word "good", skipping over words such as "goods" and "goody". You can also use the Special list to include paragraph marks and other symbols in your search and replace text.

When you want to find a word or phrase without necessarily changing anything, you will want to click Home ⇨ Find, which opens the Navigation pane. When you type your search text here and click Results, Word highlights every occurrence and lists a summary in the pane. Click the up and down arrows to scroll through the list. If you want to refine your search, click the arrow in the search box for a menu of options. Refer to Figure 15, below.

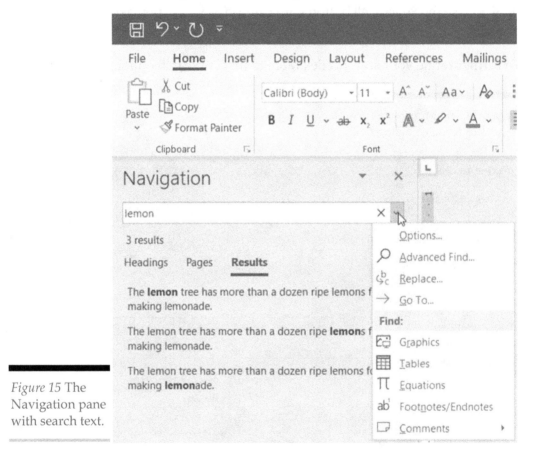

Figure 15 The Navigation pane with search text.

TIP If the Find and Replace commands aren't visible on the Home tab, click the Editing group arrow to access them in a menu.

Smart Lookup

A third tool for improving your content is Smart Lookup, a reference tool that allows you to do research right from within a document. You will find this command when you right-click a word or phrase. Selecting the command opens a Smart Lookup task pane with Internet links and related information.

Chapter 3
Formatting a Document

A document's format has as much impact on the reader as the message you're trying to convey. Formatting is broken down into character, paragraph, and page formats.

Character Formats

Character formats include typeface, point size, and type style. Together these formats refer to a *font*. Calibri 11 point regular is the default Word font where Calibri is the name of the typeface and 11 is the point size. Type styles include Regular (no emphasis), **bold**, *italic*. You can also apply effects such as underline, ~~strikethrough~~, super^{script}, color, highlight, and more. Word provides dozens of typefaces — it's up to you to choose the one that's appropriate and effective for your audience.

TIP Typefaces are classified as serif (with small lines at the ends of a letter) and sans serif (without small lines). Body text is usually easier to read in a serif font, while titles stand out when in a sans serif font. This text, for example, has Book Antiqua serif body text and Verdana sans serif headings.

TIP There are 72 points to an inch. A common standard is to make headings and titles at least 2 points larger than body text.

TIP Carefully choose effects. Underline may lead a reader to think you are providing a link, and too many colors can be confusing.

To apply character formats to an open document:

1. Select the text to format (pg. 17).
2. Click commands in the Font group on the Home tab (Figure 16, pg. 24). Note that some commands have an arrow to click for additional options (Figure 17, pg. 24).

   Or

   Click the Font dialog box launcher ⬚ in the Font group on the Home tab and then set options (Figure 16, pg. 24).

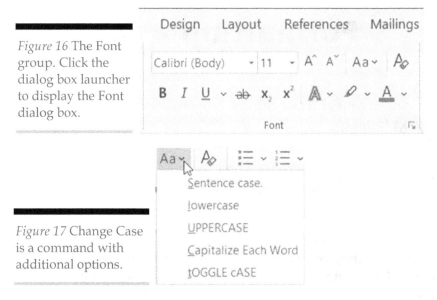

Figure 16 The Font group. Click the dialog box launcher to display the Font dialog box.

Figure 17 Change Case is a command with additional options.

Or

Click commands on the mini toolbar (available when you use the mouse to select text). (Figure 18.)

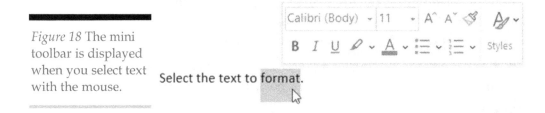

Figure 18 The mini toolbar is displayed when you select text with the mouse.

TIP To remove all character formats from selected text and restore default settings, click Home ⇨ Clear All Formatting A.

TIP When you want to change the fonts for the entire document at once, click Design ⇨ Fonts.

Paragraph Formats

A *paragraph* is any amount of text that ends with a paragraph marker. A paragraph can be several lines in length or less than one line. Paragraph formats are used to control text alignment within a page, space between lines of text, space before or after a paragraph, indents, tab stops, and the appearance of a list. Both the Home tab and the Layout tab have Paragraph groups of commands.

TIP With paragraph formats, ScreenTips are especially helpful and some even offer advice on when to use a format as in Figure 19 below. You need only point to a paragraph command to display its ScreenTip (if yours don't pop up, change your preferences in File ⇨ Options ⇨ General).

TIP When you need to set several different formats for a paragraph, it is usually faster and easier to use the Paragraph dialog box (Figure 20, pg. 26).

Alignment

Alignment refers to the way text lines up between the right and left edge of a page. Text can be left aligned, right aligned, center aligned, or justified.

To change paragraph alignment in an open document:

1. Place the insertion point in the paragraph to format. If you want to format two or more adjoining paragraphs, then select them together.

2. Click an alignment command ≣ ≣ ≣ ≣ in the Paragraph group on the Home tab (Figure 19). (Hover on an alignment button to see the ScreenTip).

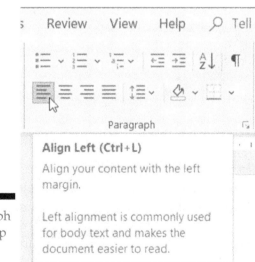

Figure 19 The Paragraph group with a ScreenTip showing.

Or

Click the Paragraph dialog box launcher in the Paragraph group on the Home tab and then choose an Alignment option (Figure 20, pg. 26).

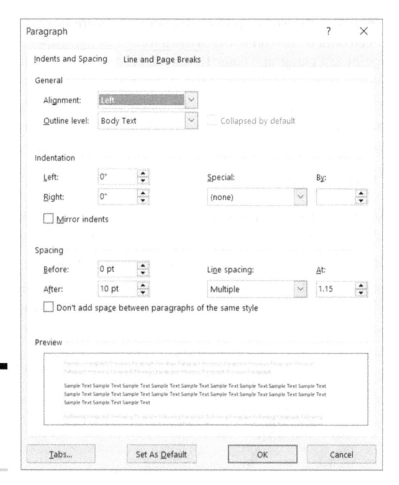

Figure 20 Click the dialog box launcher in the Paragraph group to display the Paragraph dialog box.

Indentation

Indentation refers to the distance a paragraph is from the margin. Use the Decrease Indent and Increase Indent commands on the Home tab when you want to quickly change the left indent of a paragraph. If you want to specify a right indent as well as a left, you will need to use the Left and Right options in the Paragraph dialog box (Figure 20, above) or on the Layout tab. A quote is an example of a paragraph that is often indented on the both the left and right.

If you want to see exactly where an indent will align with respect to the page, then use the *indent markers* on the ruler. When you drag a marker, a dotted line appears showing the placement. The ruler indicates the width of your page with gray areas for the margins. You can drag markers inside these areas (Figure 21, pg. 27).

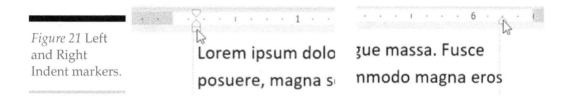

Figure 21 Left and Right Indent markers.

TIP If the Ruler is not showing, click View ⇨ Ruler.

The Special option in the Paragraph dialog box (Figure 20, pg. 26) has First line and Hanging options. Just as it sounds, First line moves only the first line of a paragraph in to create a *first line indent*. The Hanging option leaves the first line in place while pushing the remaining lines in to create a *hanging indent*. Type or select a value in the By box to adjust the indentation amount.

If you want to visually set indents, drag the First Line Indent marker or Hanging Indent marker on the left side of the ruler (Figure 22).

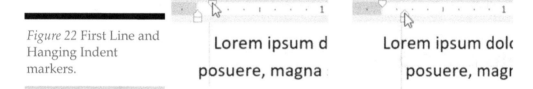

Figure 22 First Line and Hanging Indent markers.

When setting indents, be sure you first place the insertion point in the paragraph to be formatted or select multiple paragraphs before formatting.

Paragraph and Line Spacing

To adjust space above and below a paragraph, click the Paragraph dialog box launcher and enter values in the Before and After options (Figure 20, pg. 26). Before and After options are also on the Layout tab.

If you want to control the space between lines within your paragraph, then use the Line spacing option in the Paragraph dialog box (Figure 20, pg. 26). The Line and Paragraph Spacing command on the Ribbon can also be used. Click the command button arrow for a menu of choices, as shown in Figure 23 on pg. 28.

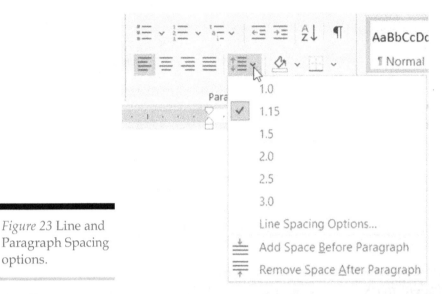

Figure 23 Line and
Paragraph Spacing
options.

TIP When you want to change paragraph spacing for the entire document at once, click Design ⇨ Paragraph Spacing.

Tabs and Tab Stops

Tabs and tab stops are used to exactly position text within a line and are often used to align data into columns, as in Figure 24.

Figure 24 Tab aligned text
with custom tab stops.

Body of Water	Date	Temp. °F	Notes
Lake Okeechobee	3/2/19	75	Freshwater
Atlantic Ocean (Miami)	3/10/19	74.2	Salt Water
Gulf of Mexico (FL Panhandle)	3/5/19	63	Salt Water

In a new document, default tab stop positions are at every half inch (0.5", 1.0", 1.5", and so on). When you press the Tab key, any text to the right of the insertion point is moved to the next tab stop. However, this may create odd alignments, as in Figure 25 on pg. 29, until custom tab stops are set, as in Figure 24 above.

Figure 25 An example of tab
separated text without custom stops.

Figure 25 An example of tab
separated text without custom stops.

Body·of·Water	→	Date→Temp.·°F	→	Notes¶
Lake·Okeechobee	→	3/2/19·75	→	Freshwater¶
Atlantic·Ocean·(Miami)	→	3/10/19	→	74.2 → Salt·Water¶
Gulf·of·Mexico·(FL·Panhandle)	→	3/5/19·63	→	Salt·Water¶

Tab stop alignment can be left, center, right, decimal, or bar. Figure 24 uses right tab stops for the dates, decimal tab stops for the temperature data (notice that even the column title is decimal aligned), bar stops between temperature and notes, and left stops for the notes. The bar stop puts a vertical line at the tab stop position but does not require a Tab character for alignment.

TIP Use tabs, not spaces, to align text. Tab stops align tabs at an exact location, whereas spaces are adjusted proportionately within a line of text and will vary in width.

To create tab stops and align text at the stops with tabs:

1. Type the information for your table, pressing the Tab key once between items and pressing the Enter key to end each line. Your data will not appear aligned until after you set stops. Refer to Figure 25 as an example.

2. Place the insertion point in the paragraph to format. If you want to set tab stops for two or more adjoining paragraphs, then select them together. In Figure 25, for example, you would need to select the four paragraphs together.

3. Click the tab selector located above the vertical ruler until you display the desired tab stop type for the first tab stop. A ScreenTip indicates the tab type. Refer to Figure 26.

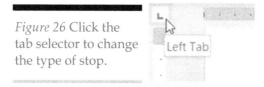

Figure 26 Click the
tab selector to change
the type of stop.

To align the data in Figure 25, for example, click the tab selector until the Right Tab ⌐ is displayed because this is the first type of tab stop to set. (Refer to the ruler in Figure 24, pg. 28.)

4.   Click in the gray area at the bottom of the horizontal ruler to insert the tab stop. You can drag the stop to any position on the ruler after it has been placed. To set the first tab for the data in Figure 25, pg. 29, for example, you will click on the sixth tick after the 2 on the ruler (Figure 24, pg. 28).

5.   Repeat steps 3 and 4 for each additional tab stop.

TIP If the Ruler is not showing, click View ⇨ Ruler.

TIP To remove a tab stop, drag it off the Ruler.

Besides setting an alignment for a tab stop, you can indicate a *tab leader*, which is a character that fills tab space. For example, leaders are used to add periods (.......) between text and a page number in a table of contents. To specify a leader, click Tabs in the Paragraph dialog box (Figure 20, pg. 26) and then specify a Tab stop position, select an Alignment, and then select a Leader (refer to Figure 27, below). You can also double-click an existing stop on the ruler to display the Tabs dialog box.

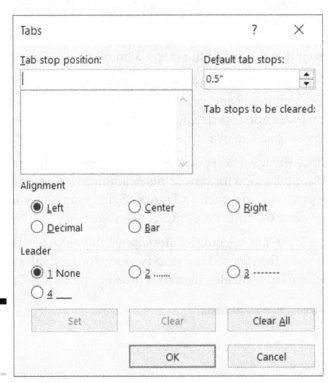

Figure 27
The Tabs
dialog box.

TIP When you want to apply character formats to just a single column of data in a tabbed table, press and hold the Alt key while dragging the mouse pointer over the column. This method selects a vertical column of text, allowing you to apply character formats to just that column.

TIP Tables (Chapter 5) are another way to align and organize data.

TIP A first line indent, not a tab, is the appropriate way to indent the first line of a paragraph.

Creating Lists

Lists present information in an organized way. A *bulleted list* is a good choice when a list contains items of equal importance. *Numbered lists* are used when items should be considered in a specific order, as in the steps on this page. Use the Bullets, Numbering, and Multilevel List commands on the Home tab to format your text into a list (Figure 28, pg. 32).

To create a list:

1. Type the items for your list into separate paragraphs. (Each item should end with a paragraph marker.)

2. Select all the list paragraphs together.

3. If the items are an ordered list, click Home ⇨ Numbering or click the Numbering arrow to choose a number style.

   Or

   If the items have equal priority, click Home ⇨ Bullets or click the Bullets arrow to choose a bullet symbol (Figure 28, pg. 32).

   Or

   If the items have multiple levels, click Home ⇨ Multilevel List and then select a list style or use commands at the bottom of the menu to define a new list style.

   Or

   Click list commands on the mini toolbar (available when you use the mouse to select text).

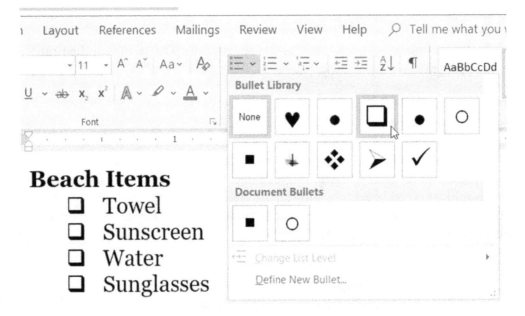

Figure 28 Click the arrow
on a list command to
display a menu of options.

4. If necessary, right-click any list item for commands to adjust indents, restart your list numbering at 1, continue numbering, and to set numbering value.

Sorting Paragraphs

Paragraphs can be sorted based on the alphabetical order of the first word for each paragraph. This is useful when you want to sort rows of data or items in a list.

To sort paragraphs:

1. Select all the paragraphs to be sorted together.
2. Click Home ⇨ Sort A↓Z. A dialog box is displayed.
3. In the Sort by list, select Paragraphs, select Text for the Type, and then choose either Ascending or Descending. Select OK. The paragraphs are sorted.

Shading and Borders

The Shading and Borders commands on the Home tab are used to apply background color, borders, and a horizontal line to selected paragraphs.

Click the Shading command arrow for color options. Click the Borders command arrow and then click Borders and Shading for a dialog box with options to customize settings. Click the Options button in that dialog box to change the border distance from the edge of the paragraph.

Paste Options

When copied items are pasted, the Paste Options button is displayed. Click this button to control how formats are pasted:

You can choose to keep the source formatting, merge the formatting to match the current location, paste as a picture, or paste only text with no formats applied (from left to right).

TIP If you want to preserve the formatting for an entire paragraph, be sure to include the paragraph marker when copying. To see the paragraph marker, click Home ⇨ ¶.

Format Painter

The Home ⇨ Format Painter command is a time-saving way to create consistent formats in your document. Its ScreenTip serves as a reminder of how to use the command (Figure 29, pg. 34).

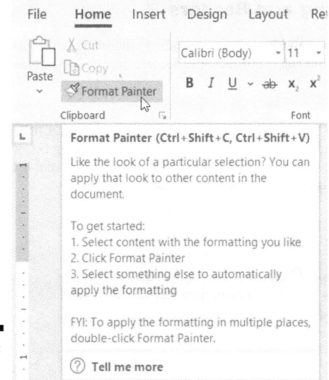

Figure 29 The Format
Painter command.

To copy and paste formats:

1. Place the insertion point in the paragraph with the formats you want to copy.

   Or

   Select the text that has the formats you want to copy.

2. Click Format Painter. When you move the mouse onto the document, the Format Painter pointer ▲*I* is displayed.

3. Scroll to the text you want to format. Click in a paragraph to apply paragraph formats or drag the I-beam pointer over text to apply character formats.

TIP If you want to apply the same formats in several locations, double-click Format Painter when copying the formats and then click in each destination location. When you no longer want to paste formats, press the Esc key.

Page Formats

Page formats include margins, vertical alignment, headers and footers, columns, page breaks, and column breaks.

Margins

Margins are the white space that extend from the defined area where content can be typed to the page edge. For example, the white areas on the top, bottom, right, and left of this page are the margins.

If margins are too narrow, a document will appear cramped and might be hard to read. There are standards, including using 1" margins all around for a typical business letter. However, even this will vary depending on your needs. Making margins slightly smaller to allow a letter to fit on one page may be more beneficial than requiring the reader to go through two pages. Also, flyers and brochures typically have much smaller margins.

The default margins in a new Word document are 1" on top, bottom, left, and right. To change your document margins:

1. Click Layout ⇨ Margins. A menu of options is displayed.

2. Click an option or click Custom Margins to display a dialog box.

TIP Margins are set for the entire document. You use indents to change the space on the left and right of an individual paragraph.

Pagination

Pagination is the process of dividing your document into pages. Word automatically ends one page and starts another when text reaches the bottom margin. But you may want to add *page breaks*, a special character that tells Word where to end a page. For example, if the first line of a list is on the bottom of a page and the remaining six lines are on the next page, you can add a page break before the first item to push it onto the next page with the rest of the list for a better layout.

To insert a page break that moves text to the next page:

1. Place the insertion point before the text that you want to move to the next page.

2. Click Insert ⇨ Page Break. A manual page break is inserted and text to the right of the insertion point is moved to the next page. If formatting marks are displayed (Home ⇨ ¶), you will see

----------------------------Page Break----------------------------¶

TIP You remove a manual page break by displaying formatting marks and then deleting the Page Break character with the Delete key.

Headers and Footers

Headers are in a special area of your document that lies within the top margin. The information in a header is repeated on every page, which makes a header ideal for displaying page numbers, titles, dates, and other references. Similarly, a footer appears in the bottom margin area. You can also choose to place information that repeats in the right or left margin area.

To add a header or footer to your document:

1. The insertion point can be anywhere in the document when you add a header or footer.

2. Click Insert ⇨ Header. A menu of formatted headers is displayed.

    Or

    Click Insert ⇨ Footer. A menu of formatted footers is displayed.

    Or

    If you want to add only a page number to your document, click Insert ⇨ Page Number. A menu of options is displayed. Scroll for options such as "Page 1" and "Page 1 of 10".

3. Click an option. The header, footer, or page number is added to your document and the Design tab is activated (Table 6, pg. 37). The Blank (Three Columns) option creates a header like Figure 30.

Figure 30

4. Click a placeholder and then type to add text. Use the Header & Footer Tools Design tab to add other information (refer to Table 6 below) and then click X Close Header and Footer to return to your document text.

5. To return to the header or footer area, double-click in the area.

TIP NEVER manually number the pages in your document. Insert a page number into the header or footer for a field code that automatically updates.

Table 6 The Header & Footer Tools Design Tab Options

Header	Click to replace the current header with a different one.
Footer	Click to replace the current footer with a different one.
Page Number	Click to replace a header/footer with a page number header/footer. Click Page Number ⇨ Current Position to insert a page number at the insertion point without replacing the header/footer. Also used to format or remove an existing page number (Figure 31).

Figure 31

Date & Time	Click to display a dialog box with date and time display options. Click Update automatically in the dialog box if you want the date and time to update every time you open your document.
Document Info	Click to insert document properties such as the file name and file path.
Quick Parts	Click for options to add document info.

Pictures, Online Pictures	Click to add graphics from your computer or clip art from the Internet. Graphics are discussed in Chapter 4.
Navigation group	Use these options to move between headers and footers.
Different first page	Select to allow the first page of your document to have a different header/footer or no header/footer at all.
Different Odd & Even Pages	Select to allow information to vary between odd and even pages. This is especially useful in very long publications where the even page displays a title and the odd page displays the author name.
Show document text	Select to display the document text as grayed out when the header/footer is active.
Header from Top Footer from Bottom	Use to adjust the placement within the margins. If you are having problems printing your header/footers, you may need to adjust the distance values.
Insert Alignment Tab	Manage the tab stops in a header/footer.
X Close Header and Footer	Click to move the insertion point back into the body of the text.

Columns

If you're creating a newsletter, brochure, or book, you'll want to consider columns.

To format your document with columns:

1. Click Layout ⇨ Columns. Options are displayed.

2. Click an option.

   Or

   Click More Columns to display a dialog box where you can exactly specify the width and spacing of your columns.

TIP Click Layout ⇨ Breaks ⇨ Column to move text after the insertion point to the next column. To remove a column break, display formatting marks and then use the Delete key to delete the Column Break character.

Section Breaks

When you want different page formats within the same document, such as one column across the top of a page and three columns for the lower two-thirds of the page, you will need to insert a section break between formats. As another example, if you want Roman numerals for page numbers in the first part of a document and Arabic numerals in the latter part, then you will need to insert a section break so that the numbering style can be changed in the headers/footers of each section.

To insert a section break:

1. Place the insertion point where you want a new section to start.
2. Click Layout ⇨ Breaks and select a section break type. Continuous is used when you want the new section on the same page, for example when you want one column at the top of a page and multiple columns on the lower page area. Next Page is needed when you want to change the format of a header or footer.

TIP You remove a section break by displaying formatting marks and then using the Delete key to delete the Section Break character.

The Page Setup Dialog box

Click the Page Setup dialog box launcher in the Page Setup group on the Home tab for additional page formats. The Margins tab is used to set mirror margins and gutters for a document with facing pages, such as a book. The Layout tab has options for vertically aligning text (Top, Center, Justified, Bottom) within a page.

Styles

A *style* is a named set of character and/or paragraph formatting choices that can be applied with a single click. The Styles group on the Home tab includes the *Styles gallery*. Click the More button ⊽ to display the full gallery.

Styles ensure a consistent look. It's also quicker to apply a style than it is to apply the same character formats and then the same paragraph formats over and over again throughout your document. The biggest advantage to using styles is that if you want to change a format, you need only change it in the named style. When a style is modified, every instance where it was applied in the document is automatically updated to match the modification.

Click the Styles dialog box launcher to open the Styles pane with styles for the current document (Figure 32). At the bottom of the pane is the New Style button along with Style Inspector and Manage Styles buttons (from left to right).

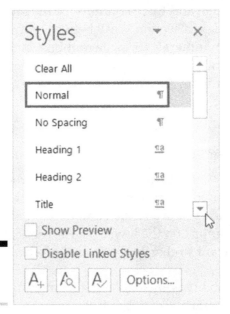

Figure 32 The Style pane.

When using styles, consider whether you need a new style or modifications to an existing style. For example, to define paragraph formats for body text you probably need only modify the Normal style. However, if you have a set of character formats in mind, then you will likely need a new character style.

To modify an existing style:

1. Right-click the style name in the Style gallery. (Click the More button to see all the styles.)

   Or

   Click the Styles group dialog box launcher ⌐ to open the Styles pane and then right-click the style name.

2. Click Modify (Modify Style in the Styles pane). A dialog box is displayed.

3. Select formats using commands in the dialog box.

   Or

   Click Format at the bottom of the dialog box. Make selections and then click OK to return to the Modify Style dialog box.

4. Verify the options at the bottom of the dialog box. IMPORTANT: In most cases, you will want to be sure that Only in this document is selected.

5.   Click OK.

To create a new style:

1.   If you want to create a new style based on the formatting you've already applied to a paragraph, then place the insertion point in that paragraph.

Or

If you want to base a new style on the formats for a set of characters, then select those characters.

2.   Click More in the Styles gallery and then click Create a Style. A dialog box is displayed. Click Modify.

Or

Click New Style A, at the bottom of the Styles task pane. A dialog box is displayed.

3.   In the Properties section of the dialog box, enter a brief descriptive Name (Keep in mind that only the first 10 characters will be displayed in the Styles gallery), select the appropriate Style type, select a base style, if desired, and then select the style for the paragraph after (the new paragraph that appears when you press the Enter key).

4.   Select formats using commands in the dialog box.

Or

Click Format at the bottom of the dialog box to select additional options. Make selections and then click OK to return to the Create New Style dialog box.

5.   Verify the options at the bottom of the dialog box. IMPORTANT: In most cases, you will want to be sure that Only in this document is selected. You may also want to be sure Add to the Styles gallery is checked.

6.   Click OK.

Navigating a Document with Styles

A document with styles is also easier to navigate because paragraphs with Heading styles are listed as links in the Navigation pane:

1.   Click View ⇨ Navigation Pane to open the Navigation pane.

2.   To jump to a paragraph, click the link in the Navigation pane.

3. To collapse an outline level in the Navigation pane, click the dark triangle next to a heading.

4. To expand a level, click the white triangle next to a heading.

5. Click Close X to close the Navigation pane.

TIP Click Pages in the Navigation pane to display clickable miniature pages for navigation.

The Design Tab

The Design tab includes options for changing Themes, Style Sets, Colors, Fonts, and object Effects. These options are primarily based on styles, so you will need to apply styles to your text and paragraphs to see the effects. Changes made from the Design tab are reflected in the styles available on the Home tab.

The Design tab is also where you'll find the Page Background group of commands.

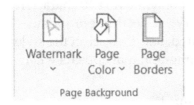

Click Watermark to add faint text or images to the background of your document pages. Commonly used watermarks are available in the Watermark gallery. If you want an image or custom text, click Watermark ⇨ Custom Watermark. To clear all watermarks, click Watermark ⇨ Remove Watermark.

Page Color changes the background color for your pages. If you want to add a pattern, such as a gradient or texture to the page color, then click Page Color ⇨ Fill Effects. Keep in mind that not all color printers print to the edges to completely change a page color.

Page Borders displays the Borders and Shading dialog box with options for border style, color, and width settings. Click Art to choose a graphical border. Use the Apply to list to place borders around every page in the document or on just pages of a section. Click the Options button to change the border distance from the edge of the page.

Chapter 4
Graphics

Graphics give your document impact and convey information. Word has options for inserting images, placing text boxes, creating WordArt, drawing shapes, and illustrating data with SmartArt and charts.

Inserting Pictures

Graphics, such as photos and clip art from your computer, network, cloud storage device, or the Internet, can be easily integrated into your Word document. Pictures and other graphics in your document are *objects* that can be formatted and edited with Word tools.

To insert and edit an image:

1. Place the insertion point where you want the image.

2. Click Insert ⇨ Pictures. A dialog box is displayed.

   Or

   Click Insert ⇨ Online Pictures to search the Internet. A dialog box is displayed.

3. For pictures on one of your storage devices, navigate to the location and then select the image. Images can be in one of many formats, commonly JPEG, TIF, or GIF.

   Or

   If you're inserting an online picture, type a search word to begin the process of finding a relevant image. (Copyright protects images from the Internet. Click the Creative Commons licenses link in the dialog box for more information.)

   The inserted image displays a Layout Options button 🖾, eight sizing handles, and a rotation handle ⟳ (Figure 33, pg. 44).

Figure 33 A selected image.

4. *Optional*. Size or rotate the image as desired (Table 7, below).

5. *Optional*. Crop the image as desired (Table 7, below).

6. *Optional*. Click Layout Options, change the image layout to floating (something other than In Line with Text), and then drag the image to the desired location (see "Picture Layout", pg. 46).

7. *Optional*. Use the Picture Tools Format tab to apply styles and adjust the image (Figure 34, see also Table 7, pg. 45).

TIP Click Insert ⇨ Screenshot to insert a screenshot from a currently open application window. Click Insert ⇨ Screenshot ⇨ Screen Clipping to insert part of an active window.

Figure 34 The Picture Tools Format tab.

Table 7 Object Editing

Size		Drag a sizing handle (the circles displayed around a selected object) to change the object size. Drag a corner handle to maintain aspect ratio. If you want the center of the image to remain in place while sizing, then press and hold Ctrl+Shift while dragging a corner handle.

‡📏 1.52"　　⋮　　🖳 0.97"　　⋮　　Size　　⌐	In the Size group on the Picture Tools Format tab, type exact dimensions in the Height and Width boxes. Click the Size group dialog box launcher ⌐ for more options.
Rotate 🔄 ◢Rotate ⌄	Drag the circular rotation handle (object must be selected) or click Picture Tools Format ⇨ Rotate.
Move ✥	The four-headed move pointer appears when you point to an object. Drag with this pointer to reposition the object.
Right-click	Right-click an object for a menu of commands for formatting, editing alt text, and controlling object-specific features.

Picture Tools Format Tab *(refer to Figure 34, pg. 44)*

Remove Background	Click to have Word make a best guess at the picture background. The command displays the Background Removal tab with options for further specifying which part of an image should be removed.
Corrections	Click for options to sharpen an image and improve contrast.
Color	Click for options to correct or recolor an image.
Artistic Effects	Click to change the look and texture of an image.
Reset Picture 🖼	Click to remove all formats.
Compress Pictures 🖼	Use this command to reduce the image sizes. File size is a consideration when emailing a document.
Picture Styles group	Point to a predefined style to preview it. Click a style to apply it. Click More ⌄ to see the complete gallery of styles. Click Picture Border, Picture Effects, and Picture Layout for more options.
Alt Text	Click to open the Alt Text pane where descriptions for your image can be added.

Arrange Group		Refer to "Arranging Objects" and Table 8, pg. 47.
Crop	⃢ Crop ⌄	Click to display cropping handles (solid black lines). Drag the handles to exclude portions of your photo. Click outside the photo after you define the crop area.

The bottom crop handle has been dragged up.

Click the Crop arrow for a menu of commands. Crop to Shape allows you to choose a shape for your image.

Picture Layout

When you insert an image at the insertion point, you create an *inline picture*. This layout means that the image is like a word in your text — it responds to word wrap, moving as text around it is added or deleted. You can also apply paragraph formats to align or indent an inline image. An inline image is not *anchored* to a position on the page.

A *floating* image can be anchored to a position on the page or dragged freely to any location, as explained in the following steps.

To anchor an image to a location on a page:

1. Click the image to select it. Handles are displayed (Figure 33, pg. 44).
2. Click Picture Tools Format ⇨ Position. A menu is displayed.
3. Click a Text Wrapping option. The image is moved and an anchor is displayed next to the floating image.

To change how an image interacts with text:

1. Click the image to select it. Handles are displayed (Figure 33, pg. 44).

2. Click the Layout Options button ⌃ . Options are displayed.

    Or

    Click Picture Tools Format ⇨ Wrap Text. A menu is displayed.

3. Choose a text wrapping option. Be sure to also select Move with text if you want your image to flow with edits to your text or select Fix position on Page if you want the image to remain fixed regardless of text flow. An anchor is displayed next to the floating image.

4. Move your now *floating* image anywhere on the page by pointing to the center (not an edge) of the image and then dragging with four-headed arrow pointer. Your image anchors wherever you move it, with text adjusting according to the selected wrapping option.

TIP If the anchor icon is not displayed, click File ⇨ Options ⇨ Display ⇨ Object anchors.

Arranging Objects

When you want to align or otherwise arrange graphics in your document, use commands in the Arrange group on the Picture Tools Format tab (Table 7, pg. 45).

Table 8 Arranging Multiple Objects

Picture Tools Format Tab Arrange Group	
Position, Wrap Text	See "Picture Layout" on pg. 46.
Bring Forward, Send Backward	Click to bring a selected object to the front of overlapping objects or send to the back of overlapping objects.
Selection Pane	Click to display a list of objects. You can click an object in the list to select it. When a graphic is hidden behind another, this is one way to select it.

Align	Click to display a menu of options for aligning one or more selected objects. To select multiple objects together, click the first object, and then press and hold the Ctrl key while you click additional objects. Note that inline objects cannot be selected for alignment.
Align ⇨ View Gridlines	Click to display a non-printing gridline behind objects for precise placement. Align ⇨ Use Alignment Guides is also useful for precise placement.
Group	Click to join two or more selected objects together. Grouped objects can be moved and formatted as a single object.

Text Boxes   This is a text box.

Text boxes are often used for pull quotes, sidebars, and other text that requires separate formatting. They can be placed anywhere in a document, and the box itself can be formatted like a graphic object.

To insert a text box:

1. Click Insert ⇨ Text Box and then pick the style you want. A text box is inserted. By default, text boxes are inserted as a floating object with square text wrapping and can be dragged anywhere on the page. Your text box will anchor itself to the position you drag it to, as indicated by the anchor icon.

2. *Optional.* If you want a different layout for your text box, click the Layout Options button. Refer to pg. 47 for more information.

3. Click once in the text box to select the placeholder text and then type your text.

4. *Optional.* Resize the text box by dragging a handle, shaping it however you want. You can change the angle of the box by dragging the circular rotation handle, or by clicking Drawing Tools Format ⇨ Rotate.

5. *Optional.* Use commands on the Home tab to format text in the text box.

6. *Optional.* Use commands on the Drawing Tools Format tab to format your text box object (Table 9, pg. 49).

TIP Click Insert ➪ Text Box ➪ Draw Text Box to draw your own text box of any size with no pre-existing text.

TIP If the anchor icon is not displayed, click File ➪ Options ➪ Display ➪ Object anchors.

Table 9 Drawing Tools Format Tab

Edit Shape	Click to change the shape or display points that can be dragged to create a customized shape.
Shape Styles group Shape Fill ˅ Shape Outline ˅ Shape Effects ˅	Point to a predefined style to preview the look of your text box. Click a style to apply it. Click More ˅ to see the complete gallery of styles. Click Shape Fill, Shape Outline, and Shape Effects for more options. Click ⌐ to open the Format Shape task pane.
WordArt Styles group	WordArt stylizes text in the text box. Point to a predefined style to preview the effect. Click a style to apply it. Click More ˅ to see the complete gallery of WordArt styles. The Text Effects ➪ Transform options usually require that you resize the text box to get the desire effect. Click ⌐ to open the Format Shape task pane.
Text group	Text Direction gives you the option of vertical text. You may need to resize the text box. Align Text is used to set the alignment of text within the text box. Create Link is used to link multiple text boxes so that text can flow from one to the next.
Alt Text	Click to open the Alt Text pane where descriptions for your object can be added.
Arrange group	Refer to Table 8, pg. 47. Refer to "Picture Layout" on pg. 45 to learn about Position and Wrap Text.
Size group	Refer to Table 7, pg. 44.

WordArt

WordArt allows you to add stylized text to your document.

To add WordArt to your document:

1. Click Insert ⇨ WordArt and then pick the style you want. (The style can be easily changed later.) A WordArt text box is inserted. By default, WordArt is inserted as a floating object that appears in front of text and can be dragged anywhere on the page. Your WordArt box will anchor itself to the position you drag it to, as indicated by the anchor icon.

2. *Optional.* If you want a different layout for your WordArt, click the Layout Options button. Refer to pg. 47 for more information.

3. Type your WordArt text. If typing does not replace the text in the box, select existing text before typing.

4. Drag a WordArt handle, if necessary, to resize the text box to accommodate your text.

    If you are typing a lot of text, you may need to reduce the font size or make the text box larger. Select text and then use the Font Size list on the Home tab to adjust type size. Or drag a handle to resize your WordArt text box.

5. *Optional.* You can change the angle of the WordArt box by dragging the circular rotation handle, or by clicking Drawing Tools Format ⇨ Rotate.

6. *Optional.* Use commands on the Drawing Tools Format tab to format your WordArt text and text box (Table 9, pg. 49).

TIP If the anchor icon is not displayed, click File ⇨ Options ⇨ Display ⇨ Object anchors.

Shapes

Shapes

You can draw shapes, such as lines, arrows, and banners, onto your document. Callout shapes also have an insertion point so that you can add text.

To add a shape to your document:

1. Click Insert ⇨ Shapes and then click the shape you want. Your pointer changes to a large crosshairs.

2. Move the pointer to the area where you want the shape and then drag to create it. By default, a shape is inserted as a floating object that appears in front of text and can be dragged anywhere on the page. Your shape will anchor itself to the position you drag it to, as indicated by the anchor icon.

3. *Optional.* If you want a different layout for your text box, click the Layout Options button. Refer to pg. 47 for more information.

4. If the shape you've added is a callout, then a blinking insertion point will be displayed. (Click the center of the callout shape if the insertion point is not displayed.) You can add text to many other shapes by using commands in the menu that appears when you right-click the object. Type the text for your shape.

   If you are typing a lot of text, you may need to reduce the font size or make the shape larger. Select text and then use the Font Size list on the Home tab to adjust type size. Or drag a handle to resize your callout.

5. *Optional.* Drag a shape handle, if necessary, to resize the shape. You can change the angle of the shape by dragging the circular rotation handle, or by clicking Drawing Tools Format ⇨ Rotate.

6. *Optional.* Select the text in the callout and use commands in the Font group on the Home tab to format text.

7. *Optional.* Use commands on the Drawing Tools Format tab to format your shape and text in the shape (Table 9, pg. 49).

TIP If the anchor icon is not displayed, click File ⇨ Options ⇨ Display ⇨ Object anchors.

SmartArt

SmartArt graphics visually convey ideas ranging from the sequences in a cycle to a family tree. They often incorporate images along with text and graphics and offer a creative, quick way to present information in an eye-catching format.

To insert a SmartArt graphic into your document:

1. Place the insertion point where you want the SmartArt graphic to appear.

2. Click Insert ⇨ SmartArt. A dialog box is displayed (Figure 35).

Figure 35 The SmartArt dialog box.

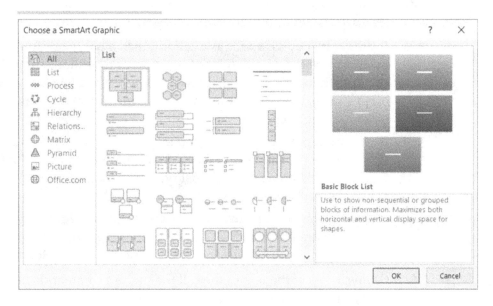

3. Choose a SmartArt graphic and click OK. You can first narrow the list by clicking a group on the left side of the dialog box.

4. By default, a SmartArt graphic is inserted as an inline object. If you want a different layout for your SmartArt, click the Layout Options button. Refer to pg. 47 for more information.

5. A SmartArt graphic displays text boxes where you need text and photo icons where you need images. Click a text box to enter your own text. Click a photo icon to display a dialog box where you can navigate to an image.

Or

Open the SmartArt graphic Text pane to enter text and select images. To open the Text pane, click the Text pane arrow on the left of a selected SmartArt graphic, see Figure 36.

Figure 36 A SmartArt graphic with open Text pane.

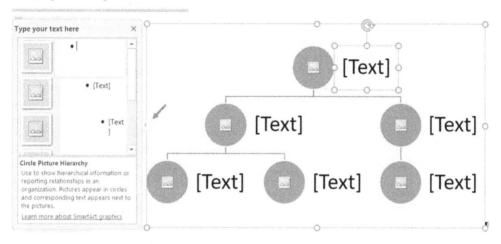

6. *Optional.* If you need to extend your SmartArt, use commands on the SmartArt Tools Design tab in the Create Graphic group. To reduce the SmartArt, delete bullets and icons.

7. *Optional.* Drag a SmartArt graphic handle, if necessary, to resize the entire object. To move your SmartArt, drag the edge of the object.

8. *Optional.* A SmartArt graphic is a collection of shapes. Right-click an individual shape in the graphic and then click Change Shape for shape options or click Add Shape for options to extend the SmartArt graphic. Drag the handles on selected shapes to rotate or size.

9. *Optional.* Use commands on the SmartArt Tools Design tab to choose layout and style options. To format individual shapes, use commands on the SmartArt Tools Format tab.

Charts

Sometimes the easiest way to explain data relationships is through a chart. Pie charts demonstrate what percentage data is of a whole. Column charts use bars to represent values, and line charts connect data points to demonstrate a trend.

To insert a chart into your document:

1. Place the insertion point where you want the chart to appear.

2. Click Insert ⇨ Chart. A dialog box is displayed.

3. Click a chart type on the left of the dialog box to display a preview. Click a variation of the chart type above the preview. Click OK. A chart is displayed with a spreadsheet containing placeholder data, as shown below.

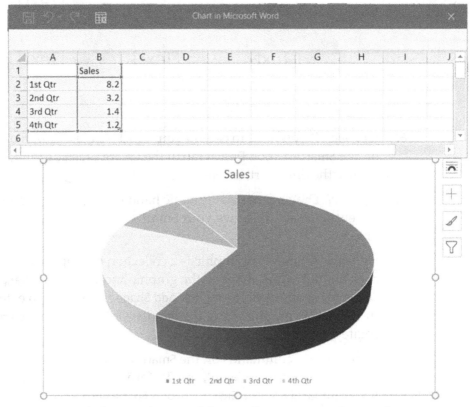

4. Click in each spreadsheet cell containing data and type your data. Delete any extra placeholder data by clicking the cell and pressing the Delete key. Drag the spreadsheet scroll bars to view other cells. Note that the pointer changes to a cross shape when pointing to a spreadsheet cell.

5. After entering the data for your chart, click X in the upper-right of the spreadsheet. At any time, you can edit data values by right-clicking your chart and then selecting Edit Data ⇨ Edit Data.

6. By default, a chart is inserted as an inline object. If you want a different layout for your chart, click the chart object and then click the Layout Options button. Refer to pg. 47 for more information.

7. *Optional.* Click the chart to display the Chart Elements, Chart Styles, and Chart Filters buttons below the Layout Options button (see left). Click any of these buttons for options to customize your chart. Drag a handle to size the chart.

8. *Optional.* A chart is a collection of objects. For example, you can select an individual pie slice and then drag it away from the other slices. Or you can use commands on the Chart Tools Format tab to format just that selected slice.

9. Use commands on the Chart Tools Design tab to choose layout and style options (Table 10, below).

10. Use commands on the Chart Tools Format tab to format individual objects (Table 10, below).

Table 10 Chart Tools Tabs

Chart Tools Design Tab

Add Chart Element	Click for commands to add, remove, and change the placement of titles, labels, legends, and more. Click More Options in any submenu to open a Format pane.
Quick Layout	Click for a gallery of suggested layouts.
Change Colors	Click for available color schemes.
Chart Styles group	Click the More button in the Chart Styles group for a gallery of styles. Point to a style to preview the effect. Click a style to apply it.
Switch Row/Column	Click to reverse the data over the axis. (Does not apply to pie charts.)
Select Data	Click to display a dialog box for changing the data range for the chart.

Edit Data	Click to display the spreadsheet associated with the chart.
Change Chart Type	Click to display a dialog box for changing the chart type.

Chart Tools Format Tab

Chart Elements list `Chart Area ▾`	Click the list arrow to display the elements of your chart. The series elements will vary. Click an element to make it active for formatting.
Format Selection	Click to open a Format pane with options for the selected element.
Reset to Match Style	Click to clear custom formatting for a selected element.
Insert Shapes group	Click a shape and then drag in the chart area to create a custom object. Refer to "Shapes", pg. 51.
Shape Styles group	Select an element and then use the Shape Styles group to customize formatting. Refer to "Shapes", pg. 51.
WordArt Styles group	Select an element and then use the WordArt Styles group to customize the look of text. Refer to "WordArt", pg. 50.
Arrange group	Click Selection Pane to open a pane where objects on the chart can be selected. Use the arrange commands to position the selected object.
Size group	Used to change the dimensions of the chart. Click the Size task pane launcher (in the lower-right corner of the group) for more options.

Chapter 5
Tables

An important consideration when creating a document is how you will present data. When you want to organize data so that it is easy to read and understand, use a Word table. In Word, you can also draw a table to create a grid for organizing a variety of elements. When used appropriately, tables add a polished, professional look to a document.

Word Tables

A *table* is organized into rows and columns where the intersection of a row and column is called a *cell*. You can place data, text, and graphics in a cell. In Word tables, the Sort and Function commands can be used to organize and summarize data.

To create a table:

    1. Place the insertion point where you want the table of data.

       Or

       If you already have text for a table (usually text that is separated by tabs), select all the text, including paragraph markers (use Home ⇨ Show/Hide ¶ to display formatting marks).

    2. Click Insert ⇨ Table and then move the pointer around the grid without clicking for a preview. Click when you have the desired table grid highlighted. An inline table is created.

       Or

       Click Insert ⇨ Table ⇨ Insert Table for a larger table. A dialog box is displayed. Type the Number of columns and the Number of rows and then select OK. An inline table is created.

       Or

       Click Insert ⇨ Table ⇨ Convert Text to Table if you have selected text for a table. A dialog box is displayed. Select or type the character that determines where one column ends and the next begins and then select OK. An inline table is created.

3. Enter data for the table by clicking in a cell and typing. Press the Tab key to move to the next cell or use the mouse to click in a cell. Press Shift+Tab to move to the previous cell.

4. *Optional*. If you want to move a table to a new location, point to the table and drag the Table Move Handle ⊞.

5. *Optional*. To change the alignment and text wrapping for a table, right-click the table, click Table Properties, and then select options on the Table tab.

6. *Optional*. Use Table Tools Design tab commands to change the overall look of the table and to format individual cells (Table 11, below).

7. *Optional*. Use Table Tools Layout tab commands to modify the table structure (Table 11, below). For example, you can add and remove rows and columns, change the width of a column, and merge cells for the title row at the top of a table.

8. *Optional*. Use commands on the Home tab to format individual cell data just like any other text. After selecting cell data, apply character formats such as bold or italic, or use paragraph formats to align cell data within a cell. Select all the table data first if you want to apply formats to the entire table (Table 11, below).

TIP Click Insert ⇨ Table ⇨ Excel Spreadsheet when you need a table that can include functions, formulas, and other spreadsheet features.

Table 11 Table Tools Tabs

Table Tools Layout Tab

Select	The Select command has a menu of options for selecting part or all of a table relative to the cell containing the insertion point. You can also make selections by pointing to the left of a row to display the right arrow shape and then clicking. Or by pointing above a column to display the solid arrow shape and then clicking.
View Gridlines	Show or hide table gridlines. Gridlines do not print and are helpful when a table does not have solid borders.

Properties	Click to display a dialog box with size, wrap, and alignment options. Click Options in this dialog box to set cell margins, cell spacing, and to turn off the option to Automatically resize to fit contents when you want your table size to remain a constant width.
Draw Table	The Draw group is covered in "Drawing Tables" later in this chapter (pg. 63).
Delete	Click for a menu of commands for deleting a cell, row, column, or the entire table. These commands are relative to the cell containing the insertion point.
Insert Above/Insert Below	Click to add a new row to your table. Alternatively, you can point to the left of a row border and then click the Insert Control to insert a row at that location.
Insert Left/Insert Right	Click to add a new column to your table. Alternatively, you can point to a column divider and then click the Insert Control to insert a column at that location
Merge group selected cells Merge Cells Split Table	Use commands in the Merge group to merge and split cells and tables. To merge adjacent cells into one, you first drag the insertion point from one cell to the last in the group to be merged and then click Merge Cells.
Eraser	Alternatively, click Eraser in the Draw group and then click the border to erase, which automatically merges cells.
	Split Table divides a table at the row containing the insertion point.
Cell Size group	Use commands in the Cell Size group to size your table. Type values in Height and Width for exact row and column sizes. You can also point to the row or column border and then drag the double-headed arrow pointer. Double-click a row or column border to get a best fit size based on your content.

Alignment group	Use commands in the Alignment group to control the way cell contents are displayed. Click Cell Margins to control the space around cell contents.
Sort and Formula	The Sort and Formula commands are covered in "Sorting Table Data" and "Using Formulas in a Table" on pg. 61.
Repeat Header Rows	Click to repeat the top row of the table at the top of each page when the table breaks across two or more pages. The insertion point must be in the first row to activate the command.
Convert to Text	Click to remove the table structure but leave the text.

Table Tools Design Tab

Table Style Options group	Click options in this group to change the options in Table Styles. For example, click Banded Columns to generate Table Styles that apply shading to every other column. Total Row generates styles that emphasize the last table row.
Table Styles group	After selecting options in the Table Style Options group, click the More button ⬇ in the Table Styles group to expand the gallery. Point to a style to preview the effect. Click a style to apply it.
Shading	Click and then click a color to change the shade in the selected cell.
Borders group	The Borders group has commands for changing border styles. After selecting an option from Border Styles, use the paintbrush pointer to click the borders to change. Press the Esc key to return to the arrow pointer.
	Selecting a Line Style, Line Weight, or Pen Color also displays the paintbrush pointer.
	Use the Borders command to change the borders of selected cell(s).
	Click the Borders and Shading dialog box launcher for options for changing the borders and shading for the entire table at once.

TIP Click Insert ⇨ Object to link or embed a spreadsheet or chart object.

TIP You may also copy and paste spreadsheet data and charts from an Excel file into a Word document.

Sorting Table Data

The rows in a table can be sorted based on text (alphabetical order), numerical values, or dates.

To sort rows:

1. Select the rows to be sorted by pointing to the left of the first row to select and then dragging the right arrow pointer to the last row in the selection. Figure 37 shows three selected rows.

HOLIDAY SALE ITEMS	
Smart Watch	$299
Board Game	$14.99
Remote-Controlled Car	$59

Figure 37 Three rows have been selected with the right arrow pointer.

2. With rows selected, click Table Tools Layout ⇨ Sort. A dialog box is displayed.

3. Select the column to base the sort, the type of sort (Text, Number, Date), and either Ascending or Descending sort order, and then OK to arrange the rows in sorted order.

Using Formulas in a Table

A table can produce calculated data by placing a formula with a function in an empty cell. Functions, for example SUM, add together the data in designated cells. (For a full list of functions, type "word functions" in the Tell Me box.)

To add a formula to a table:

1. Place the insertion point in the cell where the calculation is to appear. For a sum or average, you will want to choose the empty cell adjacent to the values that will be used for the calculation.

2. Click Table Tools Layout ⇨ Formula. A dialog box is displayed (Figure 38). It will contain a best guess formula based on values in adjacent cells, but you can change the formula.

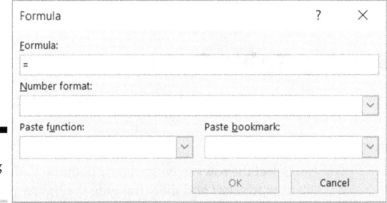

Figure 38 The Formula dialog box.

3. Delete the existing function, if necessary, leaving the equal sign.

4. Click the Paste function arrow and select a new function. The function is pasted into the Formula box. Note that a formula must begin with an =.

5. Many functions, including SUM, AVERAGE, MIN, and MAX, require positional arguments. Positional arguments can be LEFT, RIGHT, ABOVE, BELOW and combinations of these arguments (such as LEFT,RIGHT). Type positional argument(s) in the parentheses following the function name.

6. Click the Number format arrow and select the display format to use for the result of the formula.

7. Select OK. The result of the formula is displayed in the cell.

8. A formula does not automatically recalculate when cell values change. To update a formula:

    Right-click the formula and then click Update Field.

    Or

    Click the formula result and then press F9.

    Or

    Select the entire table and then press F9 to update every formula in the table.

Drawing Tables

Tables can provide a framework for layout when you want to create a document that contains multiple design elements such as logos, images, titles, and text. A cell can even contain another table, as in Figure 39.

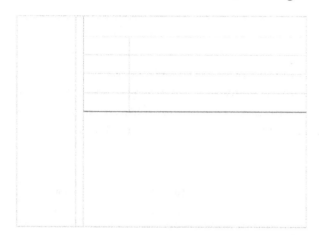

Figure 39 (top) A table created by drawing cells.
(bottom) The same table with content, cell shading, and a table style applied to the table within the table.

To draw a table:

1. Display the document page where you want to draw a table.

2. Click Insert ⇨ Table ⇨ Draw Table. The mouse pointer changes to a pencil shape when you move it onto your page.

3. Drag the pencil pointer. The perimeter of your table is created, and the Table Tools Layout tab is displayed. Any surrounding text is adjusted to make room for the table.

4. Drag the pencil pointer within the boundaries of the table to create cell borders.

5. At any time, click Table Tools Layout ⇨ Draw Table to deactivate the Draw Table command or press the Esc key. The mouse pointer changes back to an arrow shape.

6. *Optional*. To remove cell borders, click Table Tools Layout ⇨ Eraser. The mouse pointer changes to an eraser shape. Click cell borders to remove them. This command is a toggle, similar to Draw Table, and will remain in effect until you click Eraser again or press the Esc key.

7. Enter data into the table by first clicking a cell to place the insertion point and then typing or using commands to insert graphics, another table, and other objects. To move from cell to cell, use the mouse or press the Tab key.

8. *Optional*. If you want to move a table to a new location, point to the table and drag the Table Move Handle ⊞.

9. *Optional*. To change the alignment and text wrapping for a table, right-click the table, click Table Properties, and then select options on the Table tab.

10. *Optional*. Use Table Tools Design tab commands to change the overall look of the table and to format individual cells (Table 11, pg. 58).

11. *Optional*. Use Table Tools Layout tab commands to modify the table structure (Table 11, pg. 58).

12. *Optional*. Use commands on the Home tab to format individual cell data just like any other text. After selecting cell data, apply character formats such as bold or italic, or use paragraph formats to align cell data within a cell. If you've inserted objects into cells, select the object and then use the appropriate commands to format it. Select all the table data first if you want to apply formats to the entire table (Table 11, pg. 58).

Chapter 6
Mail Merge

The easiest way to provide customized letters and certificates for numerous recipients is to create a mail merge document. *Mail merge* replaces special fields with data from a list to create a personalized document. The Mailings tab is organized to take you through the mail merge process from start to finish.

Mail Merge Letters

A mail merge letter has content intended for every recipient as well as fields such as Address Block, First_Name, and Last_Name that are merged with data from a list. The steps below can be used for business letters as well as certificates and other types of documents that are to be customized.

To create a mail merge letter:

1. Create a new document.

   Or

   Open an existing document to convert to a mail merge letter.

2. Click Mailings ⇨ Start Mail Merge ⇨ Letters.

3. Click Mailings ⇨ Select Recipients ⇨ Type a New List. A dialog box is displayed.

   Or

   If you have a list of contacts stored in a spreadsheet or database, then you can use existing data. Click Mailings ⇨ Select Recipients ⇨ Use an Existing List. A dialog box is displayed. Open the list and then skip ahead to Step 9.

   Or

   Click Mailings ⇨ Select Recipients ⇨ Choose from Outlook Contacts. A dialog box is displayed. Open the contacts folder, select recipients, and then skip ahead to Step 10.

4. The New Address List dialog box contains fields that are typical for mail merge. Click Customize Columns to see the complete list of field names. A dialog box is displayed.

5.   Use the Add, Delete, and Rename buttons to customize the field names for your letter. The objective is to add the fields you will need. You are not required to delete those fields that will not be used. Click Move Up and Move Down as needed to put the field names in a logical order for data entry. Click OK. The New Address List dialog box now displays your field names in the order you've specified.

6.   Complete your recipient list by clicking in the first entry box for the first field and typing the entry. Press the Tab key to move to the next field. Continue with this process to complete the information for the first recipient. When you reach the last field, press Tab to automatically create a new recipient and place the insertion point in the first field, or click New Entry to create a new recipient row. Continue this process to enter all your data. Note that you are not required to complete every field for every recipient.

7.   Click OK. A dialog box is displayed.

8.   Save the list using a descriptive name. Once saved, the list can be used for future mail merge projects.

9.   *Optional.* Click Edit Recipient List. A dialog box is displayed. Here you can use tools to sort, filter (limit recipients to certain criteria), and even deselect duplicates.

10. Type your letter. When you come to information that is stored in your list, such as a first name, click the arrow in Mailings ⇨ Insert Merge Field and then click the appropriate field name. For a letter with an address block, click Mailings ⇨ Address Block to display a dialog box for customizing the merged address block. You may need to click Match Fields to match your specific field names to those used for the address block. The Mailings ⇨ Greeting Line command works similarly.

Figure 40 A letter with merge fields.

Dear·«First_Name»·«Last_Name»:¶

We·are·pleased·to·let·you·know·that·the·«Product_Name»·is·now·in·stock.¶

11. Format your letter. Apply character formats to fields by selecting the entire field, including the marks on either side, before selecting formats.

12. Click Mailings ⇨ Preview Results. The merge fields are replaced by the actual data from your list, similar to Figure 41 below.

    Click the forward and backward arrows in the record controls in the Preview Results group to scroll through your merged documents.

    Figure 41 A preview of two mail merge letters.

    Dear·Eda·Rosen:¶

    We·are·pleased·to·let·you·know·that·the·chip·bag·clamp·is·now·in·stock.¶

    Dear·Marty·Parker:¶

    We·are·pleased·to·let·you·know·that·the·bronze·bookmark·is·now·in·stock.¶

    You can click Preview Results again to return to the merge fields and make any changes to the letter, if needed.

13. Click Mailings ⇨ Finish & Merge to display options for completing your letter.

    Click Edit Individual Documents to display a new Word window with each merged letter separated by a page break. Click File ⇨ Print to print the letters.

    Or

    Click Print Documents to display a dialog box for selecting the letters to print.

    Or

    Click Send Email Messages to display a dialog box with options for emailing merged letters.

Store Your Address in Word

Before you start the steps for printing envelopes or labels, you may want to store your return address in Word so that it can automatically be used during the merge process:

1. Click File ⇨ Options ⇨ Advanced. A dialog box is displayed.

2. Scroll to the General options and type your return address in the Mailing address box.

3. Click OK.

Mail Merge Envelopes

Mail merge can also be used to create envelopes for the recipients in a list. If you want to create and print just a single envelope, skip ahead to "Creating Envelopes and Labels" at the end of this chapter.

1. Create a new document.

2. Click Mailings ⇨ Start Mail Merge ⇨ Envelopes. A dialog box is displayed.

3. Click the Envelope Options tab, if necessary, and then click the Envelope size arrow and choose the appropriate size.

4. In the Delivery address and Return address sections, click the Font button to change the font and style for the text. You can also change left and top offset positions. Note that the preview at the bottom of the dialog box changes to indicate the positioning.

5. Click the Printing Options tab and note the selected feed method. The selected method is based on your installed printer driver and visually explains where and how to place the envelope in the printer's feed tray. Note the feed method and then click OK. The dialog box is closed and the document changes to the size and shape of the envelope you selected. NOTE: If you stored your address in Word, it is automatically added as the return address. This can be easily changed.

6. Click Mailings ⇨ Select Recipients ⇨ Type a New List. A dialog box is displayed.

    Or

    If you have a list of contacts stored in a spreadsheet or database, then you can use existing data. Click Mailings ⇨ Select Recipients ⇨ Use an Existing List. A dialog box is displayed. Open the list and then skip ahead to Step 12.

    Or

    Click Mailings ⇨ Select Recipients ⇨ Choose from Outlook Contacts. A dialog box is displayed. Open the contacts folder, select recipients, and then skip ahead to Step 13.

7. The New Address List dialog box contains fields that are typical for mail merge. Click Customize Columns to see the complete list of field names. A dialog box is displayed.

8. Use the Add, Delete, and Rename buttons to customize the field names for your letter. The objective is to add the fields you will need. You are not required to delete those fields that will not be used. Click Move Up and Move Down as needed to put the field names in a logical order for data entry. Click OK. The New Address List dialog box now displays your field names in the order you've specified.

9. Complete your recipient list by clicking in the first entry box for the first field and typing the entry. Press the Tab key to move to the next field. Continue with this process to complete the information for the first recipient. When you reach the last field, press Tab to automatically create a new recipient and place the insertion point in the first field, or click New Entry to create a new recipient row. Continue this process to enter all your data. Note that you are not required to complete every field for every recipient.

10. Click OK. A dialog box is displayed.

11. Save the list using a descriptive name. Once saved, the list can be used for future mail merge projects.

12. *Optional.* Click Edit Recipient List. A dialog box is displayed. Here you can use tools to sort, filer (limit recipients to certain criteria), and even deselect duplicates.

13. Place the insertion point in the blank paragraph for the return address and then type the return address, if necessary. Or edit the address added by Word. (If you do not see the paragraph markers, click Home ⇨ ¶)

14. Place the insertion point in the blank paragraph for the delivery address. (If you do not see the paragraph markers, click Home ⇨ ¶)

15. Click Mailings ⇨ Address Block. A dialog box is displayed for customizing the address block. You may need to click Match Fields to match your specific field names to those used for the address block. Click OK. The address block merge field is inserted.

16. Click Mailings ⇨ Preview Results. Merge fields are replaced by actual data from your list.

    Click the forward and backward arrows in the record controls in the Preview Results group to scroll through your merged documents.

    You will need to click Preview Results again to make any changes to the envelope.

17. Click Mailings ⇨ Finish & Merge to display options for completing your letter.

    Click Edit Individual Documents to display a new Word window with each merged envelope separated by a page break. Click File ⇨ Print to print the envelopes.

    Or

    Click Print Documents to display a dialog box for selecting the envelopes to print.

    Or

    Click Send Email Messages to display a dialog box with options for emailing merged envelopes.

Mail Merge Labels

Mail merge can also be used to create labels from the information in a list. If you want to create and print labels that are all the same, skip ahead to "Creating Envelopes and Labels" at the end of this chapter.

1. Create a new document.

2. Click Mailings ⇨ Start Mail Merge ⇨ Labels. A dialog box is displayed.

3. Click the Label vendors arrow and select the type of label sheet you will be using. Scroll through the Product number list and select the product number that corresponds to your label sheet.

    Or

    Click New Label to enter the details for your label sheet. Click OK.

4. Click OK to close the dialog box. Your document layout matches your label selection. If you do not see the paragraph markers, click Home ⇨ ¶.

5. Click Mailings ⇨ Select Recipients ⇨ Type a New List. A dialog box is displayed.

    Or

    If you have a list of contacts stored in a spreadsheet or database, then you can use existing data. Click Mailings ⇨ Select Recipients ⇨ Use an Existing List. A dialog box is displayed. Open the list and then skip ahead to Step 12.

    Or

    Click Mailings ⇨ Select Recipients ⇨ Choose from Outlook Contacts. A dialog box is displayed. Open the contacts folder, select recipients, and then skip ahead to Step 13.

6. The New Address List dialog box contains fields that are typical for mail merge. Click Customize Columns to see the complete list of field names. A dialog box is displayed.

7. Use the Add, Delete, and Rename buttons to customize the field names for your labels. The objective is to add the fields you will need. You are not required to delete those fields that will not be used. Click Move Up and Move Down as needed to put the field names in a logical order for data entry. Click OK. The New Address List dialog box now displays your field names in the order you've specified.

8. Complete your list by clicking in the first entry box for the first field and typing the entry. Press the Tab key to move to the next field. Continue with this process to complete the information for the first label. When you reach the last field, press Tab to automatically create a new row and place the insertion point in the first field, or click New Entry to create a new row. Continue this process to enter all your data. Note that you do not need to complete every field for every row.

9. Click OK. A dialog box is displayed.

10. Save the list using a descriptive name. Once saved, the list can be used for future mail merge projects. The label document shows a Next Record merge field in all but the first label, similar to Figure 42.

Figure 42 New labels.

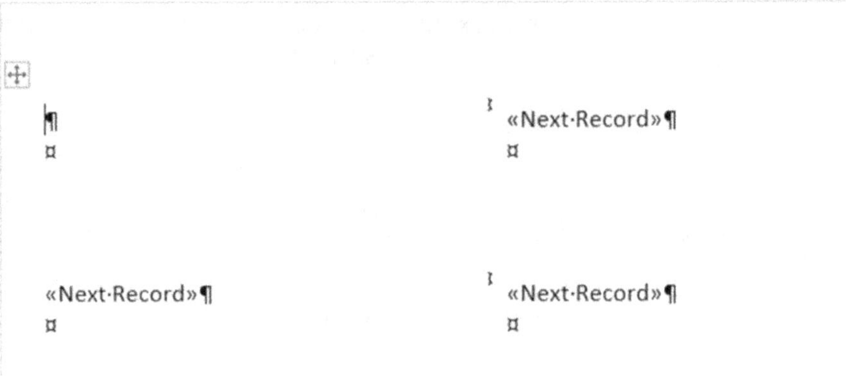

11. *Optional*. Click Edit Recipient List. A dialog box is displayed. Here you can use tools to sort, filer (limit rows to certain criteria), and even deselect duplicates.

12. Place the insertion point in the blank paragraph for the first label.

13. Click Mailings ⇨ Insert Merge Field to place merge fields in your label. Type spaces between merge fields as needed, and press Enter when you want fields on the next line. Note that in Figure 43 the first line of the label has wrapped to two lines because of the merge field lengths. The actual label may not wrap.

    Or

    If you are creating address labels, it may be easier to click Mailings ⇨ Address Block. A dialog box is displayed for customizing the address block. You may need to click Match Fields to match your specific field names to those used for the address block. Click OK. The address block merge field is inserted.

Figure 43 Labels with merge fields.

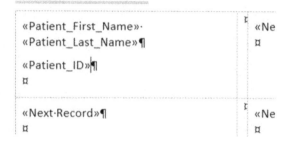

14. Click Mailings ⇨ Update Labels. The remaining labels are updated to match the first label.

15. Click Mailings ⇨ Preview Results. The merge fields are replaced by the actual data from your list, similar to Figure 44 on the next page.

Figure 44 Actual data may wrap differently than the merge fields.

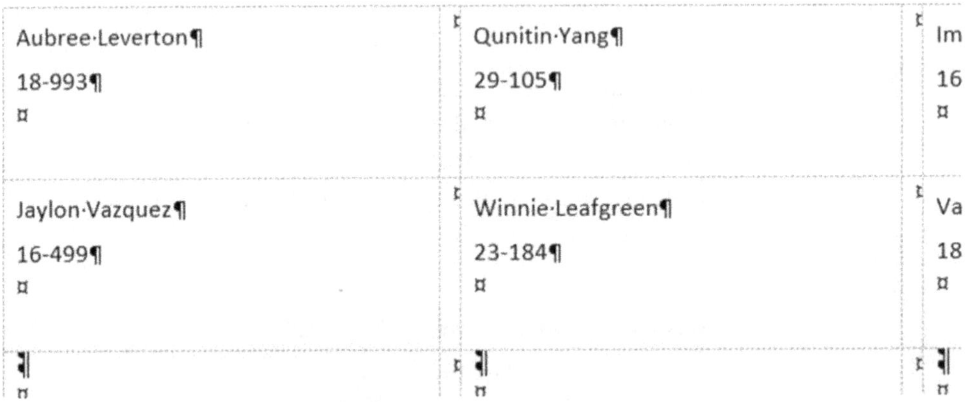

Aubree·Leverton¶	Qunitin·Yang¶	Im
18-993¶	29-105¶	16
¤	¤	¤
Jaylon·Vazquez¶	Winnie·Leafgreen¶	Va
16-499¶	23-184¶	18
¤	¤	¤

You will need to click Preview Results again to make any changes to the labels.

16. Click Mailings ⇨ Finish & Merge to display options for completing your letter.

> Click Edit Individual Documents to display a new Word window with merged labels separated by a page break if there is more than one sheet. Click File ⇨ Print to print the labels.
>
> *Or*
>
> Click Print Documents to display a dialog box for selecting the labels to print.
>
> *Or*
>
> Click Send Email Messages to display a dialog box with options for emailing the merged labels document.

Creating Envelopes and Labels

The Create group on the Mailings tab has options for creating a single envelope or a sheet of labels. If you want Word to automatically use your address as a return address, then refer to "Store Your Address in Word" on page 68 before you begin printing an envelope.

Print an Envelope

To print an envelope:

1. Create a new document.

2. Click Mailings ⇨ Envelopes. A dialog box is displayed. If you stored your mailing address in Word, then your address appears in the Return address box of the dialog box.

3. Type the Delivery address.

    Or

    Click 📖 ▾ above the Delivery address box to select an address from your address book.

4. Type or edit the Return address, if necessary.

    Or

    Click 📖 ▾ above the Return address box to select an address from your address book.

5. Click Options. A dialog box is displayed.

6. Click the Envelope Options tab, if necessary. Click the Envelope size arrow and choose the appropriate size.

7. In the Delivery address and Return address sections, click the Font button to change the font and style for the text. You can also change left and top offset positions. Note that the preview at the bottom of the dialog box changes to indicate the positioning.

8. Click the Printing Options tab and note the selected feed method. The selected method is based on your installed printer driver and visually explains where and how to place the envelope in the printer's feed tray. Note the feed method and then click OK. The dialog box is closed.

9. Click Print. The printer pauses for you to insert the envelope.

   Or

   Click Add to Document. The current document changes to the selected envelope size with the return and delivery address information. This option allows you to further edit the envelope before clicking File ⇨ Print to generate the printed envelope.

Print Labels

To print a sheet of the same label:

1. Create a new document.
2. Click Mailings ⇨ Labels. A dialog box is displayed.
3. Click Options. A dialog box is displayed.
4. Click the Label vendors arrow and select the type of label sheet you will be using. Scroll through the Product number list and select the product number that corresponds to your label sheet.

   Or

   Click New Label to enter the details for your label. Click OK.
5. Click OK to close the dialog box. Your document layout matches your label selection. If you do not see the paragraph markers, click Home ⇨ ¶.
6. Type the Address.

   Or

   Click ⬚ ▾ above the Address box to select an address from your address book.

   Or

   Click Use return address to insert the mailing address that you have stored in Word.
7. Click Print. The printer pauses for you to insert the label sheet.

   Or

   Click New Document. The current document changes to a formatted label sheet with the address information. This option allows you to further edit the labels before clicking File ⇨ Print to generate the labels.

Chapter 7
Advanced Document Features

Documents that go beyond a letter or a flyer often incorporate features such as a cover page, blank pages, a table of contents, drop caps, bookmarks, citations, and hyphenation. Development of longer documents can be made easier with outlines, tracking changes, collaboration, and the Ink Editor. This chapter serves to introduce you to these features and a few others. For further in-depth coverage of a feature, type the topic in the Tell Me box and then select the related Get Help command.

Ink

You can add your own freehand drawings, text highlighting, ink strokes, and math to a document. You can also use the Ink Editor to edit a document.

To add ink to a page:

1. Click Draw ⇨ Draw (or Draw with Touch) and then click a drawing tool in the Pens group. Refer to Figure 45, pg. 78. NOTE: If the Draw tab is not available, click File ⇨ Options and then click Customize Ribbon. Select the Draw tab and click OK.

2. *Optional*. In the Pens group, click the pen arrow and select a new thickness and color.

3. *Optional*. Click Draw ⇨ Drawing Canvas to add a box for drawings.

4. Use the mouse or other device to draw on the page or in the drawing canvas.

   Press the Esc key when you want to revert to the arrow pointer. The inked annotation is an object. Pointing to it changes the mouse pointer to the four-headed arrow pointer.

5. *Optional*. To erase ink, click Draw ⇨ Eraser and then click the inked area to remove. Click Eraser again or press the Esc key to stop erasing.

6. *Optional.* Click an inked object (with the four-headed arrow pointer) to select it and then use commands in the Drawing Tools Format tab, Table 9, pg. 49, to change the color or thickness.

Figure 45 The Draw tab.

Table 12 Draw Tab

Tools	Draw and Eraser are toggles. Click once to activate the command. Click a second time or press the Esc key to deactivate.
Pens group	Click a pen or add a new pen to change your drawing tool.
Ink Editor	Click to activate. Once activated, circle text to highlight, cross out text to delete it, draw a curve to join words, split words by drawing a vertical line at the divide, draw a caret ∧ and then write or type the word to insert, or draw a backwards shape to move text after to a new line. *Works best with touch devices and digital pens.
Ink to Shape	Click before or immediately after drawing if you want Word to convert your drawing to a standard shape. Word 365 only.
Ink to Math	Click to display a dialog box where you can draw a formula or other mathematical annotation. Use the tools in the dialog box to edit. Click Insert in the dialog box to place the mathematical symbols at the insertion point. See also "Inserting Equations" on page 87.
Drawing Canvas	Click to create a box for drawing. The canvas is an object that can be moved anywhere in the document.

Viewing a Long Document

The View tab has options that are helpful when working on a long document.

Table 13 View Tab Window Group

Navigation Pane	Select to display an outline based on Heading styles.
Read Mode	Click to hide the Word window and display a full-screen version of your document with arrows on the right and left for navigating through the pages. Press Esc to return to the Word window or use commands in the View menu displayed in the upper-left of the screen.
Print Layout	Shows how your document will appear when printed.
Zoom	Click to display a dialog box for choosing how to display your document in Print Layout view.
Multiple Pages	Click to display multiple pages in the window.
Window group	Commands used to view different parts of your document at the same time. This is useful when making edits.

Cover Page, Blank Page, and Drop Cap

A *cover page* serves to title your document and provide author and publication information. The Cover Page command is a quick, easy way to add a first page that has some basic formatting you can customize. Alternatively, you can add a blank page at the beginning of your document and create your own cover page from scratch.

To add a preformatted cover page to your document:

1. Click Insert ⇨ Cover Page. A gallery of options is displayed.

2. Click a cover page. A new page with formatting has been added to your document.

3. Click a placeholder and type to insert your own text.

To add a blank page to your document:

1. Place the insertion point where you want to insert a blank page. If the blank page will be a cover page, place the insertion point before the first character of your document.

2. Click Insert ⇨ Blank Page. A blank page with a page break is added to your document.

A *drop cap* emphasizes the first character of a paragraph to indicate the start of a document, section, or chapter.

To create a drop cap:

1. Place the insertion point in the paragraph to contain the drop cap.

2. Click Insert ⇨ Drop Cap. A menu is displayed.

3. Click the desired drop cap style.

   Or

   Click Drop Cap Options. A dialog box is displayed where you can customize your drop cap.

Bookmarks, Hyperlinks, and Cross-References

The Navigation pane allows you to quickly jump to headings in a document. If you want to be able to navigate to additional places in a document, then you add bookmarks. A *bookmark* adds a location that you can jump to with the Home ⇨ Find ⇨ Go To (Ctrl+G) command.

To add and jump to a bookmark:

1. Place your insertion at the position you want to bookmark.

   Or

   Select text that you want to bookmark. When you later jump to the bookmarked text, it will be selected.

   Or

   Select a graphic to bookmark.

2. Click Insert ⇨ Bookmark. A dialog box is displayed.

3. Type a descriptive name that begins with a letter and does not contain spaces.

4. Click Add. The dialog box is closed.

5. Click Home ⇨ Find ⇨ Go To (Ctrl+G). A dialog box is displayed.

6. In the Go to what box, select Bookmark. The Enter bookmark name list displays a bookmark name.

7. When you have numerous bookmarks, click the Enter bookmark name list arrow and select the desired bookmark.

8. Click Go To. Your document is scrolled to the position of the bookmark, selecting text or graphics if they were selected when the bookmark was created.

TIP Click Insert ⇨ Bookmark for options to delete a bookmark or jump to (go to) a bookmark location.

TIP Bookmarks are also used in eBook publications to specify locations such as the beginning of a book and the table of contents.

When you publish a document in PDF format, hyperlinks to locations within the same document provide a navigational tool for the reader. You can link text or graphics to headings and bookmarks.

To insert a hyperlink to a location within the document:

1. Format your document with Heading styles and add bookmarks, if necessary.

2. Scroll to the location to create the hyperlink.

3. Select the text or graphic you want to use as the link. (This may require that you type text or insert a graphic.)

4. Click Insert ⇨ Hyperlink or right-click the selected text or graphic and click Link. A dialog box is displayed.

5. Click Place in This Document. Headings and bookmarks are listed.

6. Click the location for the hyperlink and verify the Text to display.

7. *Optional.* Click ScreenTip to enter text that will display when the user hovers their mouse over the link.

8. Click OK. The selected text or graphic is now a hyperlink. You can test the link by pressing Ctrl while clicking once on the link.

A *cross-reference* can link to numerous types of locations in a document, including headings, bookmarks, numbered items, and tables. When you create a cross-reference, a field code is inserted based on what you choose to reference. For example, you can link to a numbered item and choose to create a link that references its page number. If the item moves to a different page, the cross-reference automatically updates. Cross-references can also be used to insert text from a selected location to the reference location.

To insert a cross-reference:

1. Type the text that will begin the cross-reference. For example, "Please refer to the directions on page ".

2. Click Insert ⇨ Cross-reference. A dialog box is displayed.

3. Click the Reference type list arrow and select a location in your document. Note that the reference must exist before you can create the cross-reference.

4. Click the Insert reference to arrow and select what will be inserted in your document.

5. Click the reference in the For which box, which displays available references based on your selection in the Reference type list.

6. Select Insert hyperlink to display a link to your cross-reference.

7. Click Insert. The results of the field code are displayed. If the field code is displayed rather than the results, press Alt+F9 or right-click the code and select Toggle Field Codes.

Hyphenation

Hyphenation refers to the process of using hyphens (-) to split a word across lines of text. You can get more evenly spaced text with increased readability if you hyphenate a long document. This is most applicable to a document with justified text.

Hyphenation should be performed with care. A little extra space between words is better than half a word on the last line of a paragraph or three lines in a row that end in hyphens.

To hyphenate a document:

1. Place the insertion point at the very beginning of the document.

83

2. Click Layout ⇨ Hyphenation ⇨ Manual. A dialog box is displayed prompting you to choose the recommended hyphenation for a word.

3. Click Yes to hyphenate the word at the blinking position indicated in the dialog box. The word is hyphenated, and the process continues to the next candidate for hyphenation.

    Or

    Click No to skip the word. The original word and wrap remain and the process continues to the next candidate for hyphenation.

4. When Word is done checking your document for hyphenation candidates, a dialog box alerts you. Click OK.

5. Review your document. If you want to remove a hyphen, simply delete it.

TIP Avoid Layout ⇨ Hyphenation ⇨ Automatic because you will not be able to individually remove hyphens, if needed.

TIP To reverse all hyphenation, click Layout ⇨ Hyphenation ⇨ None.

Table of Contents

The Table of Contents, or TOC, appears at the beginning of a document and lists headings and their page numbers. If you export a document to PDF, the TOC entries will be active links. You can automatically generate a TOC if you've applied heading styles to your document.

To create an automatically generated TOC:

1. Format your document with Heading styles as appropriate, if necessary.

2. Place your insertion point where you want the TOC inserted. (Insert a blank page after the title page, if necessary.)

3. Click References ⇨ Table of Contents ⇨ Automatic Table 1 (or another option from the gallery). A TOC is generated with the title "Contents".

4. Click the TOC. Controls are displayed above the TOC.

- Click [icon] for options to change the TOC format or to remove the TOC.
- If you make changes to your document, click Update Table or press F9 to update titles and page numbers.

5. Press and hold the Ctrl key while you click a TOC entry to scroll to that heading.

TIP Word can also automatically generate an index. Select text for indexing and click References ⇨ Mark Entry. After marking the document, click References ⇨ Insert Index.

Outline View

Outline view is helpful when editing the structure of a long document. In this view, headings and content are displayed as bullet points that can be easily moved around.

To use Outline view:

1. Open a document that has been formatted with Heading styles.
2. Click View ⇨ Outline. The document is converted to an outline and the Outlining tab on the Ribbon is displayed.
3. Click the icon next to a heading or paragraph. The heading and its paragraphs are selected.
   - Click the right and left arrows in the Outline Tools group to demote or promote the outline level for the selected text.
   - Click the up and down arrows in the Outline Tools group to move selected text.
4. Click Close Outline View to return to Print Layout.

Citations and Bibliographies

Citing sources and creating an accompanying bibliography, referencescreating, or works cited page are common for research papers. Word makes this task easier with built-in resource styles and an automated bibliography generator.

1. Click References ⇨ Style and then select the citation style.
2. Place the insertion point where you want the citation.

3. Click Insert Citation ⇨ Add New Source. A dialog box is displayed with the recommended fields for the entry.

   Or

   If you've already added the source, it will appear in the Insert Citation menu. Click the existing source. A citation is inserted. Skip ahead to step 5.

   Or

   If you don't yet have the source information, but want to mark the text for citation, then click Insert Citation ⇨ Add New Placeholder. A dialog box is displayed. Type the label and select OK before skipping ahead to step 5.

4. Complete the entries for the dialog box. If you have additional information, click Show All Bibliography Fields and complete as many of those entries as you have data for. Select OK.

5. Repeat steps 2 through 4 for every reference needed in your paper.

6. Before generating the bibliography, click each placeholder citation, if any, and then click the arrow and select Edit Source. A dialog box is displayed. Refer to Step 4 to complete the source information.

7. Place your insertion point where you want the bibliography inserted. (Add a blank page at the end of the document, if needed.)

8. Click References ⇨ Bibliography ⇨ Bibliography (or another option from the gallery). A bibliography is generated with a title.

   Or

   Click References ⇨ Bibliography ⇨ Insert Bibliography if you want to insert citations without adding a formatted title.

9. Click the Bibliography. Controls are displayed above.

   - Click 🔲▾ for options to change the bibliography format or to convert the bibliography to static text.
   - Click Update Citations and Bibliography to update entries when your document is edited.

TIP Click References ⇨ Manage Sources to add previous citations to your current document.

TIP Be sure to double-check your citation format against current standards.

TIP Type "bibliography" in the Tell Me box and then select a Help topic for more information.

TIP Type "APA bug" in the Tell Me box and select the first Help topic for information on how to correct a Word bug with the APA 6th Edition citations.

TIP The References tab also has commands for inserting a table of authorities.

Footnotes and Endnotes

Footnotes and endnotes provide another way of referencing sources or providing information about text.

To insert a footnote or endnote:

1. Place the insertion point at the footnote or endnote location.

2. If you want to add a footnote, click References ⇨ Insert Footnote. A number is added at the location and the insertion point is moved to the bottom of the page.

    Or

    If you want to add an endnote, click References ⇨ Insert Endnote. A number is added at the location and the insertion point is moved to the end of the document.

3. Type the footnote of endnote information. Double-click the footnote or endnote mark to return to the previous document location.

4. If you want to delete a footnote or endnote, select the footnote or endnote in the text and then delete it. The corresponding entry is deleted.

TIP To navigate footnotes and endnotes, click References ⇨ Next Footnote or click the arrow in Next Footnote and click Next Endnote.

Inserting Equations

Word provides commonly used equations ready to insert. For custom equations, Word now includes LaTeX math syntax.

To insert an equation:

1. Place the insertion point where you want to insert an equation.

2. Click the Insert ⇨ Equation arrow. A gallery is displayed.

3. Click an existing equation. It is inserted. Skip ahead to step 5.

    Or

    Click Insert New Equation. An equation placeholder is inserted, and the Equation Tools Design tab is displayed.

4. Type numbers, click symbols, and select structures to generate the equation you need. Structures have placeholders that you click to type numeric values.

5. Click the equation to select it, if necessary, and then click the arrow to display a menu of display options.

6. If you want to delete an equation, select it and then press Delete.

TIP Click Insert ⇨ Equation ⇨ Ink Equation to draw your own equation.

Creating a Template

Templates save time when creating a similar document over and over again. For example, if you have a weekly meeting agenda, then you can create your agenda from a template that already contains your headings and titles and even the unchanging bullet items.

To create a template file:

1. Create a new Word document and add the basic content that you will need in every document based on this one.

    Or

    Open an existing document that you would like to create a template from.

2. Click File ⇨ Save As.

3. Click This PC.

4. Click the box with Enter file name here and type a new name for the template file.

5. Select Word Template (*.dotx) from the type list, as shown in Figure 46 below. Note that document will be saved to the Custom Office Templates folder.

Figure 46 The Save As type list.

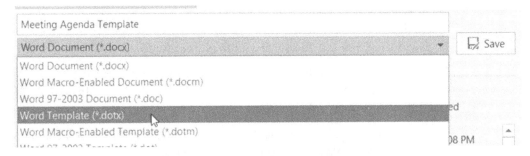

6. Click Save.

To use a template file for a new document:

1. Click File ⇨ New.

2. Above the featured templates, click Personal. Your personal template files are displayed.

3. Click a template. A new document is created based on your template.

Collaboration

Collaboration on a document allows others to contribute to development.

If you want collaborators to contribute to your document, you will need to share the document:

- Click Share in the upper-right of the Word window, upload the file to OneDrive, and then invite people through email to access the file.

- Collaborators can click Comments to open the Comments pane where they can respond to comments that have been added to the document.

For more information, use the Tell Me box to get help on "share a document".

TIP Changes are automatically periodically saved to documents stored in the cloud. Others can see updates in seconds.

TIP Click File ⇨ Options ⇨ Save and then click Embed fonts in the file before sharing.

TIP Another form of collaboration uses the Review ⇨ Compare command to compare and combine two presentations.

Tracking Changes

The Review ⇨ Track Changes command keeps track of any changes made to your document. This feature is especially useful when you want others to review and comment on your document while keeping your original content.

To track changes:

1. Click Review ⇨ Track Changes. Track Changes is a toggle and remains selected until you click it again.

2. Click the Display for Review list. Click Simple Markup to display symbols when a change has been made, No Markup to show only the revised document, All Markup for edits and strikethrough marks, or Original to see the original document. It is typical to switch back and forth among these options as you edit your text.

Figure 47 Edited text with Track Changes on and showing All Markup.

There are ~~many~~ nine new colors for the ~~updated~~ May product line.¶

3. Click New Comment when you want to add a comment bubble at the insertion point.

To review changes:

1. Click the Display for Review list. Click All Markup to display edits and strikethrough marks.

2. Click Previous and Next in the Changes group to jump from change to change to review edits.

3. Click Accept to make a tracked change and automatically jump to the next change.

    Or

    Click Reject to undo a change and automatically jump to the next change.

4. Click Previous and Next in the Comments group to scroll through the comments. Use Delete to remove a comment.

Document Inspector

The final check for a document that will be shared electronically is to remove personal information and hidden data. As helpful as it may be to wipe your document of this type data, which is referred to as *metadata*, you will also want to perform the check on a copy of your document because the metadata may not be able to be restored. The document inspector can also be used to alert you to accessibility and compatibility issues.

To remove personal information and hidden data:

1. Save your document.

2. Click File ⇨ Save As.

3. Type a new name for your document, such as My Letter Copy, and then click Save.

    Or

    Click Browse. A dialog box is displayed so that you can navigate to a new location to save a copy of your document.

4. Click File ⇨ Info and then click the Check for Issues ⇨ Inspect Document. A dialog box is displayed.

5. Read through the options and clear any content you do not want reviewed.

6. Click Inspect. A report is displayed.

7. Review the results and click Remove All where you want metadata to be deleted.

8. Click Close to remove the dialog box.

TIP Click Review ⇨ Check Accessibility to open a pane that tracks accessibility issues in your document.

Index

Word 2019 Quick Reference

from the book *Microsoft Word 2019 In 90 Pages* © Belleyre Books 2019

Document Setup

- Layout ⇨ Size to choose a page size. *p. 11*
- Layout ⇨ Orientation to choose Portrait or Landscape. *p. 11*
- Layout ⇨ Margins ⇨ Custom Margins to change space around text. *p. 35*

Document Views

- View ⇨ Navigation Pane to display an outline based on Heading styles. *p. 41, 79*
- View ⇨ Print Layout to see how your document will appear printed. *p. 9, 79*
- View ⇨ Read Mode for full-screen. Press Esc to return to the Word window. *p. 9, 79*
- View ⇨ Zoom to change magnification. *p. 79*
- View ⇨ Multiple Pages for an overall view. *p. 79*

Select & Edit Text

- Home ⇨ ¶ (Show/Hide ¶) to display formatting marks. *p. 12*
- **Click once** to place the insertion point before you type text. *p. 17*
- **Double-click** to select a word. *p. 19*
- **Drag** from one word to another to select a block of text. *p. 17*
- On the Home tab, click Cut or Copy to remove or copy selected text. *p. 18*
- Home ⇨ Paste to insert previously cut or copied text. Click Paste Options to control formats. *p. 18, 33*

Find & Replace

1. Click View ⇨ Navigation Pane.
2. Type text in the search box. *p. 22*

   Or

   Click the search button for the Replace command. *p. 20, 22*

Format Characters

1. Select text to format.
2. Click commands on the mini toolbar.

    *p. 24*

   Or

   Click commands in the Font group on the Home tab. *p. 23*

Format Paragraphs

1. Select paragraphs to format.
2. On the Home tab:
   - Click an alignment button. *p. 25*
   - Click an Indentation button or drag indent markers on the ruler. *p. 26*
   - Click the Line and Paragraph Spacing button for options. *p. 28*
   - Click in the Paragraph group and select options from the Paragraph dialog box. *p. 26*

To Copy Formats

Select the text with the formats you want to copy and click Home ⇨ Format Painter. Next, click the paragraph or text to receive the formats. *p. 34*

Set Tab Stops

1. Type text, using tabs to separate columns of text. *p. 28*
2. Select text to format.
3. Click the tab selector above the vertical ruler until the appropriate tab stop is displayed. *p. 29*
4. Click in the gray area at the bottom of the horizontal ruler to place a stop and then drag the stop to the desired position. *p. 29*

   Or

   Click in the Paragraph group and click Tabs to display a dialog box to set stop position, alignment, and leader. *p. 30*

Create a List

1. Type the list items, pressing Enter at the end of each item. *p. 31*
2. Select list items to format.
3. Click Home ⇨ Numbering to create a numbered list. *Click the button arrow for number options. *p. 32*

   Or

   Click Home ⇨ Bullets to create a bulleted list. *Click the button arrow for bullet options. *p. 32*
4. Right-click an existing list for commands to modify the list.

Microsoft and Microsoft Word are registered trademarks of the Microsoft Corporation.

Pagination & Breaks

- Insert ⇨ Page Break to move text after the insertion point to the next page. *p. 35*
- Layout ⇨ Columns to divide a page into columns. *p. 38*
- Layout ⇨ Breaks ⇨ Column to move text to the next column. *p. 38*
- Layout ⇨ Breaks and then select a section break to divide a document to allow for different section formats. *p. 39*

Headers & Footers

1. Click Insert ⇨ Header/Footer. To insert just a page number, click Insert ⇨ Page Number. *p. 36*
2. Select an option.
3. Click the placeholders to edit them. Use the Header & Footer Tools Design tab to add information. *p. 37*
* To create different headers/footers in the same document, use section breaks and clear the Link to Previous button on the Header & Footer Tools Design tab.

Styles

- Click a style on the Home tab in the Styles group to apply a named set of formats to the selected paragraph. *p. 39*
- Click the Styles dialog box launcher to open the Styles task pane:
  - Right-click a style name and click Modify Style to edit it. *p. 40*
  - At the bottom of the task pane, click New Style A₊ to add a new style. *p. 41*

Pictures

1. Click Home ⇨ Pictures/Online Pictures. *p. 43*
2. Navigate to the image file or search for one online.
3. Drag the image handles to size it or use commands on the Picture Tools Format tab. *p. 44, 45*
4. Click Picture Tools Format ⇨ Wrap Text and select an option to change how your image interacts with text.

Text Boxes

1. Click Insert ⇨ Text Box and then choose a style or select Draw Text Box to create your own. *p. 48*

2. Click once inside the text box to type your text. Use commands on the Home tab to format the text.
3. Drag the border to move the text box. Drag a handle to size it.

Tables

1. Click Insert ⇨ Table and point to the number of rows and columns. *p. 57*
2. Drag the Move handle ⊞ to move a table to a new location.
3. Click in a cell and type to enter text. Press Tab to move to the next cell.
4. Use commands on the Table Tools Layout tab to change the structure or right-click in a table for related commands. *p. 58*

Mail Merge

1. Create a new document or open an existing document. *p. 65*
2. On the Mailings tab:
   a. Click Start Mail Merge ⇨ Letters.
   b. Click Select Recipients ⇨ Type a New List. (or click Select Recipients ⇨ Use an Existing List or Select Recipients ⇨ Choose from Outlook Contacts.)
   c. Click Customize Columns and add, delete, and rename fields specific to your document. Close the dialog box when fields are complete.
   d. Click in the recipient list and type data. Close the list when complete.
   e. Click in your document and click Insert Merge Field wherever you want data from your list. Format the inserted fields to match your document.
   f. Click Preview Results to view your document with actual data.
   g. Click Finish & Merge for options to edit, print, or email your merged documents.
* See pages 71–76 to mail merge envelopes and labels and to create single envelopes and repeating labels.

Microsoft and Microsoft Word are registered trademarks of the Microsoft Corporation.

www.ingramcontent.com/pod-product-compliance
Lightning Source LLC
Chambersburg PA
CBHW080539060326
40690CB00022B/5181